IMAGES
of America

SANTA CLARITA
VALLEY

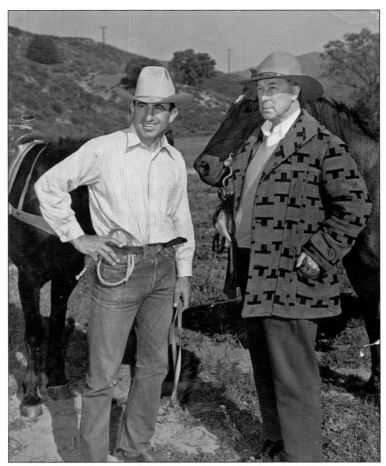

No two men better capture the soul of the Santa Clarita Valley than Hall of Fame rodeo cowboy Andy Jauregui (left) and legendary silent-film star William S. Hart. Jauregui was famous for decades as one of the top rodeo personalities in the country. Jauregui's ranch was next door to today's Walt Disney's Golden Oak ranch, and back when, a Who's Who of Hollywood stayed with the lanky cowboy. Everyone from Clark Gable to Errol Flynn took "cowboying" lessons from him. Besides being one of the top silent-film stars in the world, William S. Hart built an epic castle in the heart of downtown Newhall. Today the castle is located within a Los Angeles County Park. Hart is credited with creating the original, and authentic, screen cowboy persona, based in part on the great characters of Shakespeare and on Hart's real life as a cowboy. Around the globe, America's cowboy image, as a black-and-white moral frontier hero, comes in large part from "Two-Gun" Bill Hart. (Courtesy Noureen Jauregui Baer, who adopted the book's author, John Boston.)

ON THE COVER: With its true-life Wild West heritage, it is only fitting that moviedom chose the Santa Clarita Valley (SCV) as a favored shooting location. For more than a century now, the SCV has been a second Hollywood. Thousands of films, from major motion pictures to mouthwash commercials, have been filmed here. With its other worldly vistas, deadly outlaws like Tiburcio Vasquez and producers of old-time B-movie oaters (Westerns) found Vasquez Rocks a perfect place for ambiance. From left to right, movie legends Bob Steele, Hoot Gibson, and Ken Maynard stare toward a distant horizon in search of bad guys. (Courtesy Leon Worden and the SCV Historical Society.)

IMAGES
of America

SANTA CLARITA VALLEY

John Boston and the
Santa Clarita Valley Historical Society

ARCADIA
PUBLISHING

Copyright © 2009 by John Boston and the Santa Clarita Valley Historical Society
ISBN 978-0-7385-6938-3

Published by Arcadia Publishing
Charleston, South Carolina

Printed in the United States of America

Library of Congress Control Number: 2008940086

For all general information contact Arcadia Publishing at:
Telephone 843-853-2070
Fax 843-853-0044
E-mail sales@arcadiapublishing.com
For customer service and orders:
Toll-Free 1-888-313-2665

Visit us on the Internet at www.arcadiapublishing.com

*To all Time Ranger saddlepals, the Santa Clarita Valley
Historical Society, to Ruth Newhall, Jerry Reynolds, A. B.
Perkins, Leon Worden, and the thousands who made and
passed along the colorful fabric and soul of our valley.*

CONTENTS

ACKNOWLEDGMENTS

Certainly no story about the "Little Santa Clara River Valley" can be told without those making history and those keeping it.

I am humbled by the chain of good people, stretching back centuries, who have passed along the culture, fable, wit, and courage along with their questionable decision-making. There are the usual suspects within the endless spectrum of the Santa Clarita Valley of pirates, volunteers, resume-building bureaucrats, and saints to thank. At the top of the list is Leon Worden, who, for decades now, has joined historians A. B. Perkins and Gerald "Jerry" Reynolds in quietly and tirelessly adding to the growing coffers of the SCV's historical fortune.

Someone wise once said that we only die after the last person remembers us. I owe Pat Saletore, executive director of the Santa Clarita Valley Historical Society, a huge debt. She not only managed to dig up most of these dusty and fading memories but also labored like a benign shaman to scan the images for posterity.

I have lived most of my life in this valley and marvel at how much the people give to the community. The SCV Historical Society is a marvelous group composed of Johnny and Jane Appleseeds, who are planting history for future generations and sharing the SCV's rich life—with just enough wickedness to make them interesting.

The "mighty" *Signal* is that swashbuckling little daily newspaper now nearly a century old. For a quarter century, during the valley's most dynamic change, the "Holy Trinity" at the periodical was Scott, his wife, Ruth, and their son, Tony Newhall. They reminded us, daily, of the paper's motto: "Vigilance Forever." That translated to actively caring for our history.

What follows is but a thumbnail of the story of the Santa Clarita Valley. With but 200 or so graying photographs and a few thousand words, it's impossible to capture the myriads of tales, legends, statistics, and deeds of so many. A proper volume would be encyclopedic. For those who do not appear in the following pages, do not despair. The saga of the SCV is ongoing.

Thanks to these remarkable people. The Santa Clarita shall not be forgotten.

INTRODUCTION

How far back do you have to go to find out who you are? Geologists pondered, that 4.6 billion years ago, perhaps the moon broke away from a wiggling earth where Santa Clarita's zip code rests today. With a few less zeroes, millions of years ago, a huge sea broke through its banks and washed into an ocean filled with rich minerals—gold, zinc, copper, quartz, titanium, uranium. Miners would harvest the riches, making the Santa Clarita Valley (SCV) one of the West's biggest boom areas. The remains of dinosaurs and Buick-sized Pleistocene creatures helped fill vast lakes of underground petroleum. In Placerita Canyon, some of the planet's purest oil—a white, nearly clear substance—still bubbles from a secret pool.

Geology and geography define who we are. The *Anasazi*—ancient big-game hunters—left little record of their centuries here. They quietly disappeared around 400 AD. About 50 years later, a migrating and war-like band of *Shoshone* traipsed all the way from the Midwest to call Santa Clarita their home. Over the years, they metamorphosed into an isolated tribe of two dozen villages, scattered over about 100 square miles.

The ancient ones who left no name, the near-nude *Tataviam*, the Spanish, and the Americans who followed all lived in a common geographic location, which each developed as a center for transportation and commerce. It began with ancient Native American trade routes stretching as far away as Mexico, Colorado, and even Catalina Island. The Spanish widened these hiking trails for horse and wagon. The Americans completely changed the landscape by linking north-south and east-west rail lines in the SCV, followed by roads for the California Aqueduct. The Santa Clarita Valley is often referred to as the "navel of the universe" because it is the center of all these ancient-to-modern trade routes going back thousands of years, and also because, from a Zen standpoint, it is considered to be a centered place.

Travel was not without its cost. For more than a century, road agents plagued the trails. One of the West's biggest range wars was staged in Castaic at the dawn of the 20th century. In my short lifetime, I have seen a staggering change: there are now more churches than saloons in Santa Clarita. This was a home for Tiburcio Vasquez, who still holds the honor of being the center of attention of the largest manhunt in California history. Joaquin Murietta was beheaded just up the road. Cave Johnson Couts noted in his diary about nests of cattle rustlers hiding in tall grass or behind the countless opportunities of ambush.

We like our canyons in Santa Clarita. They are perfect for hiding moonshine. Road agents in the 1930s used to ambush drivers making hairpin curves on the old Ridge Route. With the freeway close to everywhere, we were a favored dropping-off spot for corpses, and Richard John Jensen, serial killer, stalked hitchhiking victims along dark and lonely roads.

For decades, community leaders have offered essentially the same version of a yoga-like speech, demanding that those starved for entertainment look to the past, be in the moment, yet keep an ear to the future. Sometimes a small story shouts volumes over a bloated speech.

In the 1930s, an all-points bulletin was put out for a heinous murderer. A man matching his description was spotted boarding a train headed for the Saugus Station. Word got out and, in less than an hour, nearly 100 armed deputies and vigilantes were waiting on the wooden platform.

Seeing the mob, the man bolted across the street, behind the Saugus Café. Bullets darkened the air. Some are still plastered over in the historic little eatery's walls. Miraculously, he was not shot. As they dragged him to the patrol car, the felon confessed. He had never killed anyone, but he had stolen a car in Bakersfield several months earlier and thought the battalion of roughnecks was just for his benefit. He congratulated the vigilance committee for having so much community spirit and for their "stand on law and order."

Over the years, the SCV has managed rather nicely in a functional schizophrenia. We have many names. This valley has been called Rancho San Francisco, Valencia, Kent, Newhall-Saugus, Newhall-Saugus-Valencia, Valencia Valley, Canyon County, Canyon Country, Camulos, and the Soledad Township (an actual, 1,000-square-mile rural township with borders stretching to Tejon, Palmdale, Chatsworth, and Fillmore). In the 1930s, Arthur Buckingham Perkins, the town's young historian, kiddingly called us the Little Santa Clara River Valley. Los Angeles's last wild river, the Santa Clara, runs through, although Congressman Buck McKeon (R) once dismissed it as an apologetic line of dust. Twice we failed at becoming our own county. We failed more than that trying to become our own city. But, in 1987, locals formed their own version of the Boston Tea Party and broke away to form the City of Santa Clarita. It's been, with a few footnotes, a marvelous experiment.

The St. Francis Dam was built along the point where three earthquake faults meet and against a mountain wounded by an ancient slide. It burst in 1928, sending cows, boulders, and 500 people to their watery deaths. Next to the San Francisco earthquake and fire, it was the second worst disaster in California history.

Prohibitionists tried to start a colony here in the late 1800s. Their leader, Henry Clay Needham, though swearing off booze, was addicted to seeking public office. Thrice he ran for the presidency, along with taking a swing at the governor's mansion and a seat in the U.S. Senate. He fared pretty well for a third-party candidate, except in the SCV. He never carried his own valley.

We are an unusual place. There were Bigfoot sightings here in the 1940s and 1970s. Addi Lyon, noted community leader, reported seeing a pterodactyl flying about. That was in the 1880s. Gerald Ford ditched speaking at our prestigious CalArts campus. The same morning, he had to be sworn in as president when a disgraced Richard Nixon stepped down. Patty Hearst reportedly hid out here. So did gangster Bugsy Siegel in his second home on Arcadia Street near his neighbor, Charles Lindbergh, who was a few doors down from W. C. Fields.

Some of the silver screen's most famous people called the SCV home. William S. Hart lived in a mansion overlooking Newhall. Hart was the top Western-box-office star of the day. With a good wind and a nice driving wood, "Two-Gun" Bill could hit the house of the next top box-office hero: Tom Mix. Hoot Gibson owned a rodeo ranch. Harry Carey had a 3,000-acre spread in San Francisquito Canyon, manned by Navajo Indians.

The SCV had its own nuclear missile silo that today is a resting spot for condors. The world's two largest grizzly bears were reportedly shot here (as well as the state's biggest timber wolf). There are prettier places on the planet but few that epitomize the Zen term "suchness."

Today the greater Santa Clarita Valley encompasses the communities of Newhall, Saugus, Valencia, Canyon Country, Castaic, and Val Verde. Acton and Agua Dulce are sort of teetering on being our "19th province," but historically they are still close kin.

In just a blink, the population of the valley has mutated from a few thousand to nearly a quarter million. Its business used to be cattle, farms, oil, and movies (literally thousands have been filmed here the past century). Today Santa Clarita is part bedroom community (nearly a third of the population are students), part light-to-medium industry-based.

What has not changed is this indefinable bond and affection we have for one another. Unlike many other growing suburbs, the people of the Santa Clarita Valley stay connected. As one old-timer grumpily put it, "You can't throw a rock any day of the week and not hit a charity event." We're good medicine for one another.

—*Vayan con Dios*,
John Boston
The Time Ranger

One

A MILLION YEARS, THEN VOICES

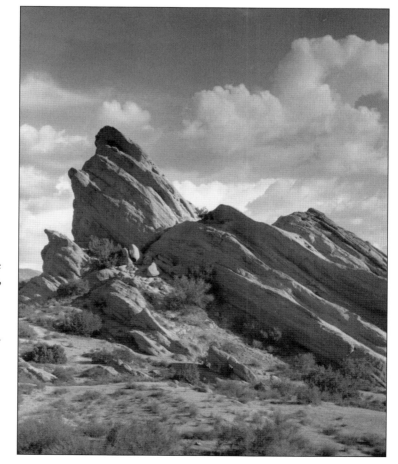

Imagine eons without the sound of a human voice. Primitive man reached the Santa Clarita Valley about 18,000 years ago. Some lived at Vasquez Rocks, which today is a Los Angeles County Park. Grinding holes and bunks can still be seen. A developer tried to buy Vasquez Rocks and put up condos. He wanted to paint, in giant white letters, the new name: Moon Valley. (Courtesy SCV Historical Society.)

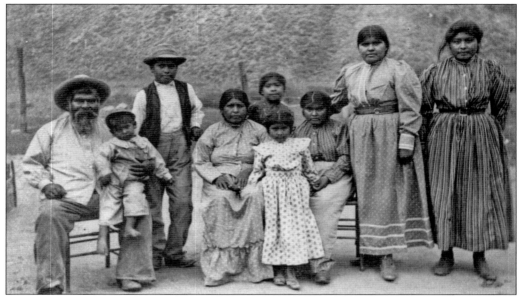

About 7,000 years ago, the climate was cooler. One can still see remnants of those ancient conifer forests atop Newhall Pass and Bear Divide. Around 450 AD, the Tataviam, a branch of Shoshone, migrated to the SCV. Geographically isolated, they spoke with a guttural clicking sound. Juan Jose Fustero and his family were the last of the peoples. (Courtesy SCV Historical Society.)

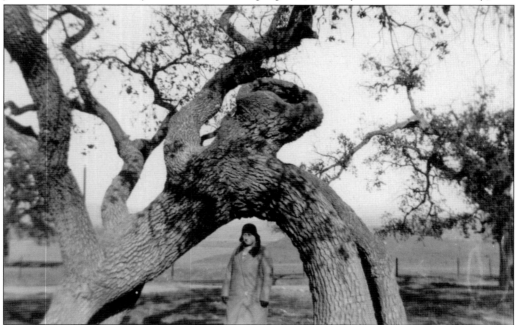

Some old-timers call the SCV "the navel of the universe." It was the hub of ancient, vast Native American trade routes. Chinese general Homer Lea, in the early 20th century, named the SCV one of the top 10 military targets on earth because of the key intersection of roads and rails. This "Marker Tree" is still in Stevenson Ranch and was bent by Native Americans as a road sign. (Courtesy SCV Historical Society.)

The Tataviam were the SCV's dominant Native American peoples, and Juan Jose Fustero was the last full-blooded male. He was a gifted horseman. Barely 5 feet tall, he weighed 350 pounds and sported a protruding hernia. Locals believed Fustero found Joaquin Murrieta's lost treasure because he would show up in town regularly with $20 gold pieces. In 1921, his family found his heat-bloated corpse and a small fortune underneath. (Courtesy SCV Historical Society.)

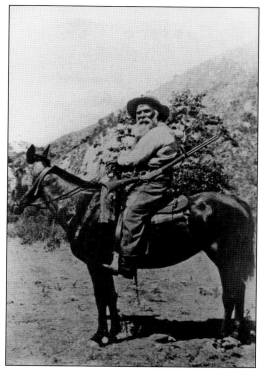

Sinforosa Fustero (right) was mother to Juan Fustero and believed to be the last full-blooded Tataviam woman. In her final years, around 1910, she lived in a tent on Walnut Street. The Tataviam's homeopathic cures included swallowing red ants to cure dysentery and the yerba santa plant as a painkiller. Like most Southern California tribes, they rarely fought against other Native American communities. (Courtesy SCV Historical Society.)

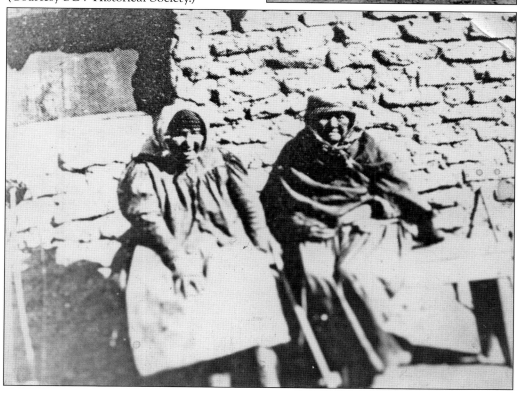

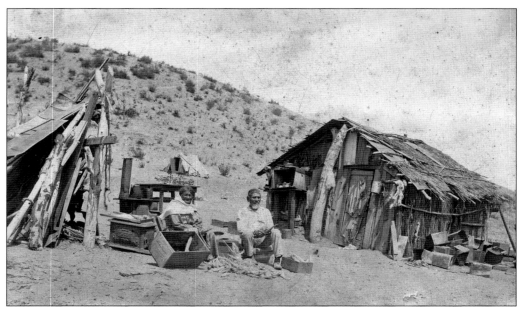

Because of a misunderstanding in the 1920s, the extinct local Native Americans were called *Alliklik*. Translated, it means "naked stuttering dirt-eater." In the 1970s, it was discovered that the correct name is *Tataviam*— "dwellers of the sunny slope." They were scattered in about 25 semi-permanent villages. Two population figures have been given: 500 and 1,500. The Tataviam divided themselves into two clans, coyote and mountain lion. Neither could marry within their clan. The Tataviam had a creation story similar to Genesis. Fustero and his wife are seen at his lean-to in the image above. When a wickiup became too buggy, it was burned and a new one built. Fustero ended up living near Piru Creek but was cast out by religious publishing mogul David Cook, who was the author of *The Garden of Eden* and was known as the Father of Piru. Fustero and his family are seen in the image below. (Both courtesy SCV Historical Society.)

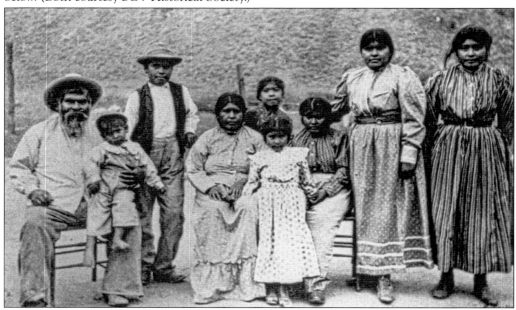

Much of what is pieced together about the Tataviam comes courtesy of teenage brothers McCoy and Everett Pyle. Near the Chiquita Canyon landfill today, they found a cave in 1884 stuffed with what was called one of the most significant caches of Native American artifacts. It is called Bower's Cave after Dr. Bowers, who bought the cache from the boys. The hundreds of items currently are stored in the Peabody Museum at Harvard University. Perhaps "Mac" suffered some Tataviam curse for raiding the tomb. When he first entered the cave, he wrote, in charcoal, "Mac Coy, 1884." He became a local lawman, and just a few years later, some local thug snuck up behind him in Castaic, put a revolver to the back of his head, and shot him to death. (Both courtesy SCV Historical Society.)

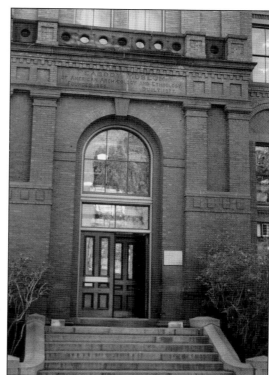

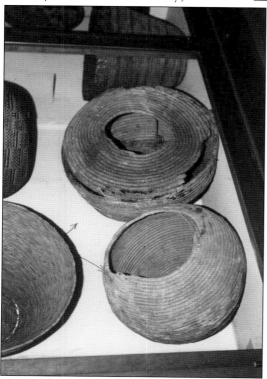

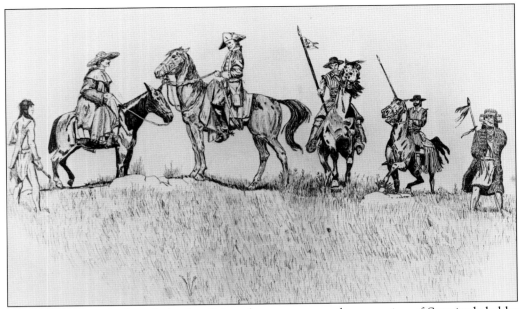

It must have been such a clash of realities when a quarter-mile procession of Spaniards led by Gaspar de Portola entered the SCV on August 8, 1769. He was on a mapping expedition. Portola was California's first governor and the first white to see the valley. An interesting tidbit is that Newhall Land executives did not realize Portola's birthplace was Valencia, Spain—the community they named Valencia after. (Courtesy Jerry Reynolds Collection.)

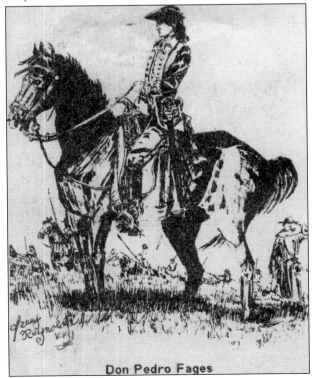

Don Pedro Fages

Also on that first trek was Don Pedro Fages. Later, he would "discover" many Southern California spots, including Soledad Canyon. California's fourth governor, he was embroiled in the state's first political sex scandal. Aided by Fr. Junipero Serra, Fages's wife tried to get him recalled for having affairs with Native American maidens. Fages tried to have Serra removed as mission president on charges of barbarous treatment of Native Americans. (Courtesy Jerry Reynolds Collection.)

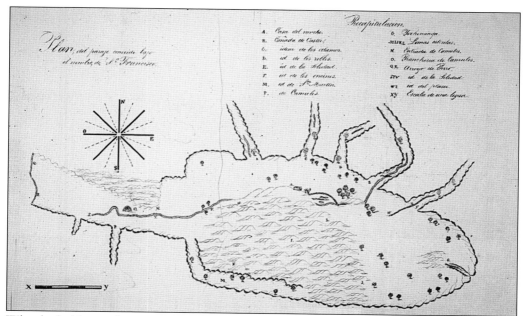

What looks like an alien cow stomach or an upside-down flea is an 1843 Spanish map of Rancho San Francisco. Those appendages show the various canyons: Castaic, San Francisquito (or Bouquet), Mint, Soledad, and Placerita. Elsmere Creek is at the bottom right. At upper left is where the Del Valle ranch house rested. (Courtesy SCV Historical Society.)

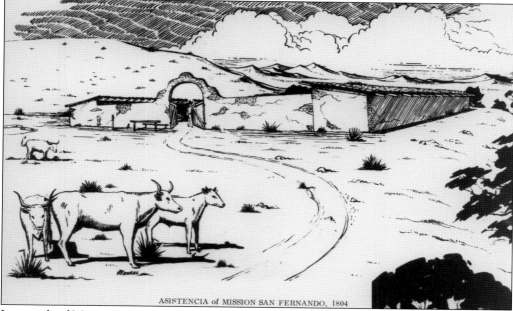

ASISTENCIA of MISSION SAN FERNANDO, 1804

Just north of Magic Mountain today was the location of the "missing" mission, Estancia de San Francisco Xavier. For years, there was debate as to whether it was an actual mission or a hub of the San Fernando Mission. In 1804, the padres learned that Francisco Avular was spreading his influence in the SCV. The Catholics built the 17-by-105-foot, five-room Asistencia to keep a foothold here. (Courtesy Adolph Henkel/SCV Historical Society.)

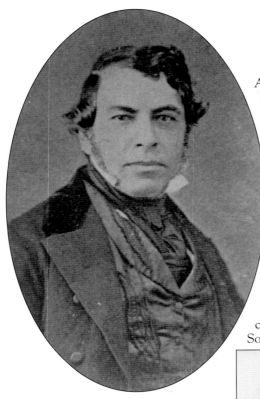

Antonio del Valle was majordomo of the San Fernando Mission, which included the SCV. Owed back wages by the governor, in 1839, Antonio swapped the IOU for the entire valley and became one of just 400 landowners in California. His son, Ignacio del Valle (left), took years to acquire most of his father's holdings. Ignacio was a Los Angeles alcalde, state official, government administrator, and wealthy landowner. The estancia would be expanded. Antonio del Valle, then his son, Ignacio, would turn it into their home. It was abandoned after the huge 8.3 Tejon Quake in 1857, and Ignacio would build up Camulos. By 1933, all that was left was a wall and glazed floor tile. Historian Arthur Buckingham Perkins (below) inspects the last of what was used by Newhall Land as a cattle-feeding bin. (Above courtesy SCV Historical Society; below courtesy A. B. Perkins.)

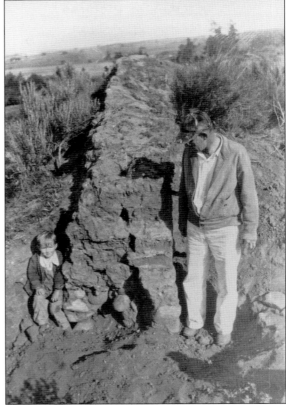

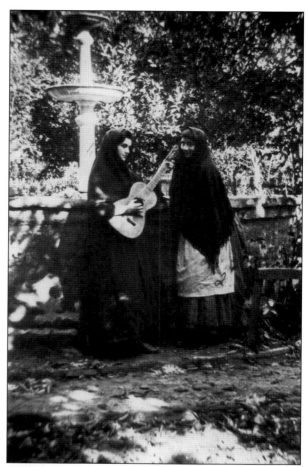

For years in the mid-19th century, Camulos would be the heartland and center of the Santa Clarita Valley. Ignacio del Valle would marry his 15-year-old fiancée Isabella and start a family. After years of fighting to keep title, Ignacio would be forced to sell his beautiful ranch (which is a state historical landmark today and fruit stand on Highway 126). But he would stay on, leasing his former lands, growing crops, raising cattle, and living comfortably—as would his relatives (about 100 of them; meals were served in shifts) until 1925. At right, beautiful Nena (left) and Susanita del Valle pose with guitars, and below, Susanita dances *la jota* with Antonio Colonel. (Both courtesy SCV Historical Society.)

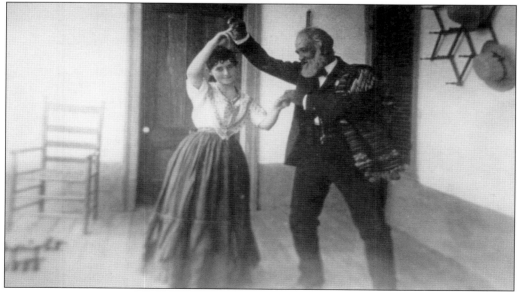

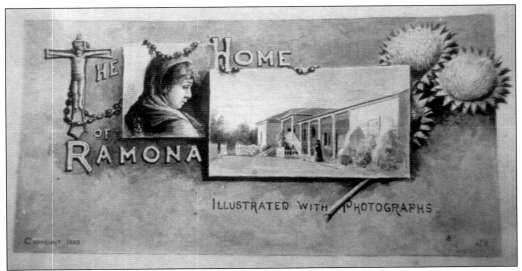

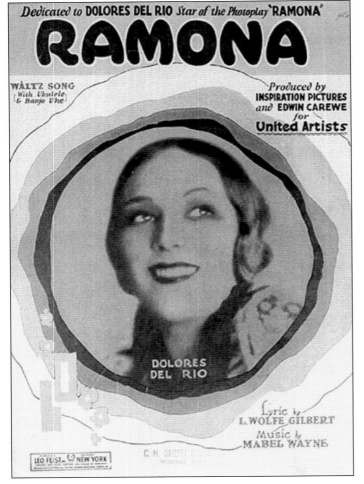

Helen Hunt Jackson's *Ramona* had a profound effect on American culture. The 1884 romantic novella painted Southern California as a Garden of Eden and helped create a real estate boom. It also changed many American prejudices against Native Americans, albeit creating a new, romantic stereotype of them as guitar-playing, Shakespeare-quoting innocents. Ramona leagues formed to discuss or debunk the story. Postcards by the tens of thousands circulated back east. Jackson's inspiration came when she stayed at the Camulos Ranch. It became a huge attraction, with trains dropping off fawning tourists. Ramona memorabilia sold like hotcakes. For a nickel, visitors could jump on the bed on which the real Ramona was born. (Both courtesy SCV Historical Society.)

Two

And the Valley Shall Never Be the Same

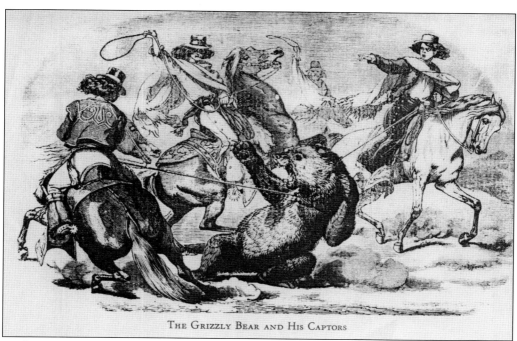

THE GRIZZLY BEAR AND HIS CAPTORS

Nothing beats a symbol for conquering Mother Nature than riding out on horseback, at night, tracking a giant grizzly bear, lassoing it, and dragging it back—alive—to the house. Vaqueros at Ignacio del Valle's Rancho San Francisco would return on moonlit nights, sometimes with a live grizzly in a large burlap bag, just for sport. From there, taming the SCV was comparatively easy. (Courtesy SCV Historical Society.)

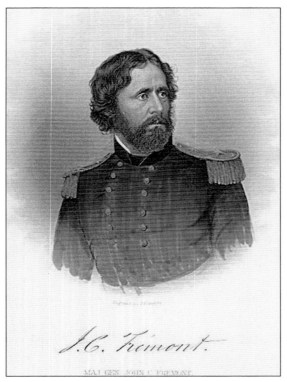

America's first Republican presidential candidate, John C. Fremont, was a frequent guest of the Santa Clarita Valley. Many still confuse Fremont Pass with Newhall Pass—the former is a bit east of the latter. Fremont squeezed seemingly 50 lives into one. He was the spearhead of Manifest Destiny and friend of Ignacio del Valle. Fremont was the very creator of the SCV's modern roads. (Courtesy SCV Historical Society.)

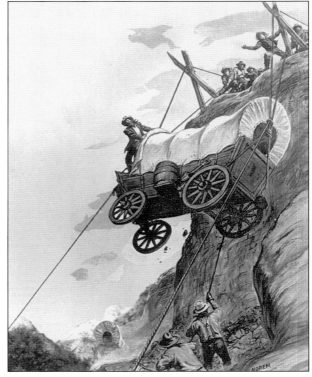

Before there was any reasonable highway in the SCV, in the 1850s, folks and things with wheels and legs on them entered and exited the SCV via Henry Clay Wiley's windlass. It would be around Beale's Cut today. Sometimes it was speculated that the windlass lowered a giant pallet, which was used to raise livestock and lower them to the neighboring San Fernando Valley. (Courtesy Jerry Reynolds.)

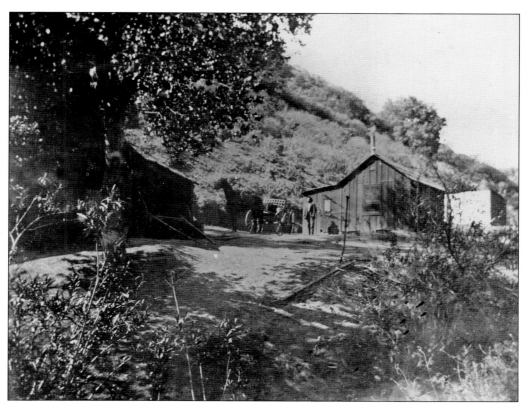

The area about where the Eternal Valley sits today used to be the center of the pre-1876 town of Santa Clarita. The place went from Lopez Station, to Wiley Station, to Lyons Station, to Andrews. The town with tavern, store, stage stop, and post office was almost called Malezewski, Andrew's last name, but the postmaster did not want to spell it. (Courtesy SCV Historical Society.)

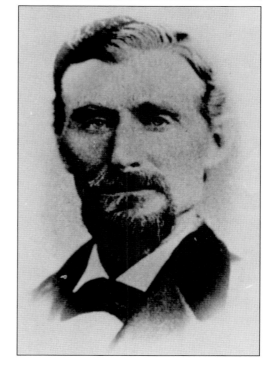

Twin brothers Cyrus (gunfighter) and Sanford (businessman) owned the Lyons Station stage depot on the east side of the valley in the 1860s. Cy (right) was a captain in the California Rangers, the unit that cleaned up bloody El Pueblo—Los Angeles—where at least a murder a day occurred. Lyons Avenue is named after the brothers. (Courtesy SCV Historical Society.)

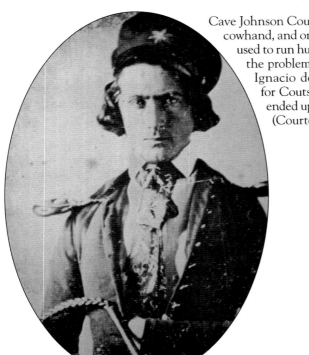

Cave Johnson Couts was a West Point graduate, explorer, cowhand, and one of California's wealthiest men. Couts used to run huge herds through the SCV and reported the problem of rustlers. He would stay with friend Ignacio del Valle. One cattle drive went bust for Couts. He ran 15,000 head to San Jose and ended up splitting $35 in profit with his brother. (Courtesy SCV Historical Society.)

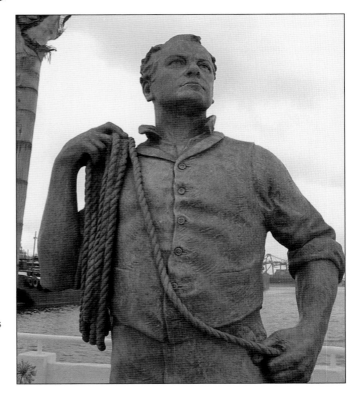

While this statue of Phineas Banning guards the Port of Los Angeles, the noted teamster made SCV history in December 1854 when he piloted the first wagon over Fremont Pass. It crashed big time. Banning's road foreman, Gabe Allen, was one of the meanest gunfighters in the area. Allen, later a Los Angeles County supervisor, would shoot Native Americans for target practice. He shot a Los Angeles roofer off a ladder to test his rifle sites. (Courtesy Leon Worden.)

One of the most robust figures in SCV history is Henry Mayo Newhall. He went from a penniless gold prospector to one of the richest men in California in a span of months. Owning blocks of downtown San Francisco and founding the H. M. Newhall Trading Company, he acquired 143,000 prime acres, including most of the SCV, which he purchased for less than $2 an acre. In 1878, he built one of the West's finest resorts. The Southern Hotel was the centerpiece of the new town of Newhall but burned down a decade later (there are talks about rebuilding it today). Newhall died in 1882 after a horse tumble in Santa Clarita. It took a year for his widow, Margaret Jane, and five sons to settle his estate and create the Newhall Land and Farming Company. (Above courtesy Tony Newhall; below courtesy Newhall Land.)

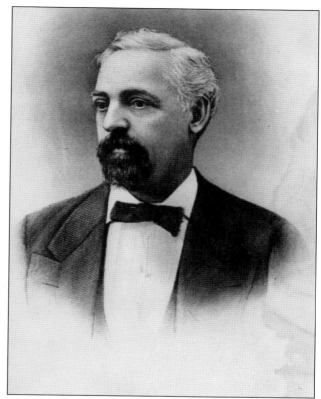

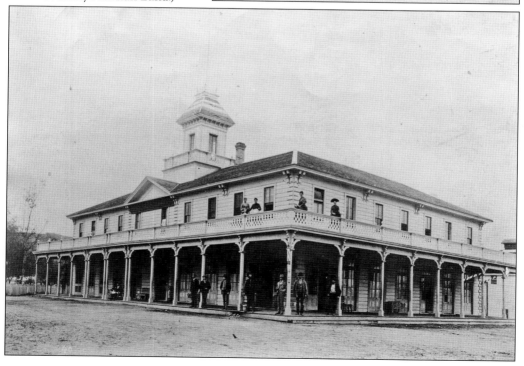

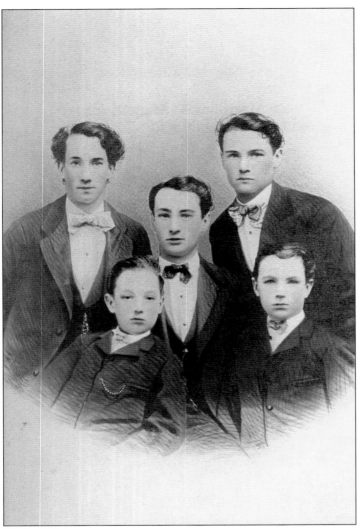

Henry Mayo Newhall, "Hank," was first married to Sarah Ann White and had two children by her. She died. Hank married her sister, Margaret Jane White, and they had three more sons (all five children are pictured at left). On June 1, 1883, the five brothers and their mother founded the NL&F Company with the offering of 10,000 shares of stock. The boys took 1,250 each and Margaret kept 2,500. The original company included 143,000 acres—or 225 square miles—of prime California real estate. The boys, at the time, were from 21 to 30 years old—not a bad inheritance for being so young. During several recessions in the 1880s, 1890s, and early 20th century, several times after forming Newhall Land, the boys tried to sell the company. During the Depression, in 1932, the entire SCV was up for sale with an asking price of $750,000. (Both courtesy Tony Newhall.)

Thomas Mitchell fought alongside Sam Houston in the Mexican-American War and in 1860 became the first white settler in Soledad Canyon. He competed with grizzlies and Native Americans in trying to keep cattle. He bought a tiny miner's cabin in Tehachapi, rebuilt it in Canyon Country, and brought his bride, Martha, to live with him in 1861. They would build a handsome house in Soledad. Their humble homestead would grow to nearly 1,000 acres. Besides farming and ranching, they, and their bees, produced 40 tons of honey a year. The couple, along with the Langs, organized the Sulphur Springs School in 1872—the third oldest school in Los Angeles County, following Acton/Agua Dulce and Los Angeles. The first classes were taught in the Mitchell kitchen. In 1886, with the help of Sanford Lyon, the current campus was built off Sand Canyon. (Both courtesy SCV Historical Society.)

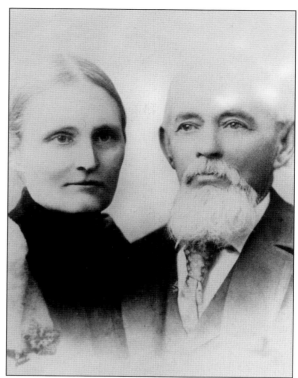

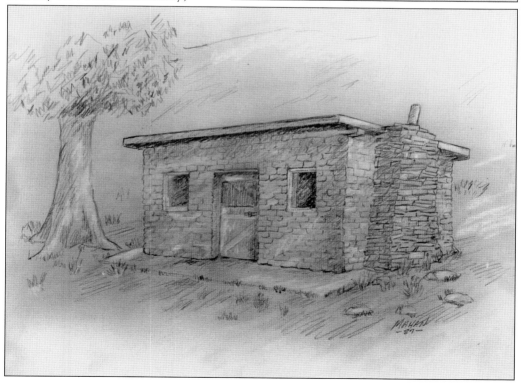

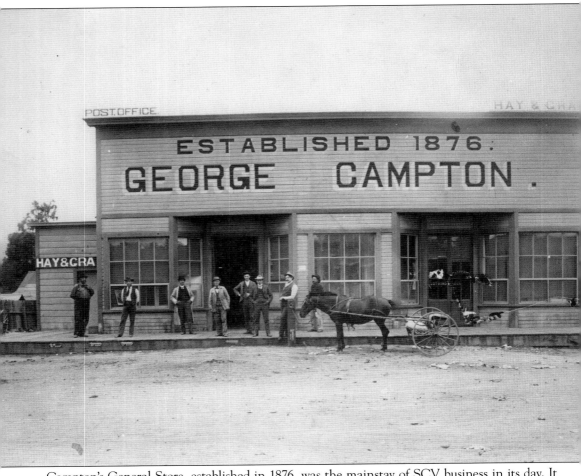

Campton's General Store, established in 1876, was the mainstay of SCV business in its day. It housed the valley's first phone in 1900. Folks would walk or ride on horseback to make or receive a call. The SCV's second phone was installed 11 years later. By 1924, the only 24-hour phone was at Wood's Garage. In 1960, the SCV became California's first rural community to switch to direct dialing. The building burned to the ground in 1961 on a night when the mercury dipped to the teens and the pipes froze. After George Campton got out of the general store and post office business, several other establishments used his building. They were Bricker's Radio Shop, McIntyre Gift Shop, the People's Market, M&N Market, a butcher shop, then finally, Hilburn's Funeral Parlor. (Both courtesy SCV Historical Society.)

Three

HEROES AND VILLAINS

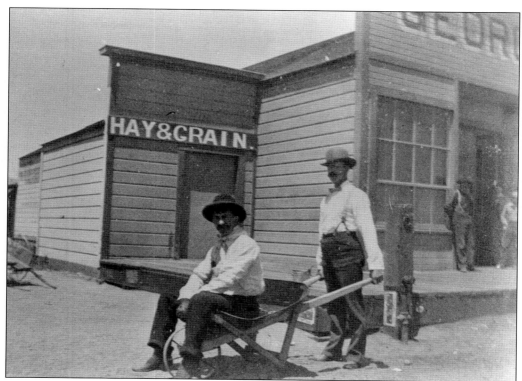

Lou Henry's father, Charles, managed gold mines in Acton. As a young girl, she played on the slag heaps. Tomboy, expert horsewoman, and taxidermist, Lou Henry would enter Stanford University in 1894 and marry a young geology student named Herbert Hoover, who became president of the United States. At a Stanford reunion, Lou was backing up and ran over young Richard Boone (*Have Gun, Will Travel*), breaking his arm. (Courtesy the White House.)

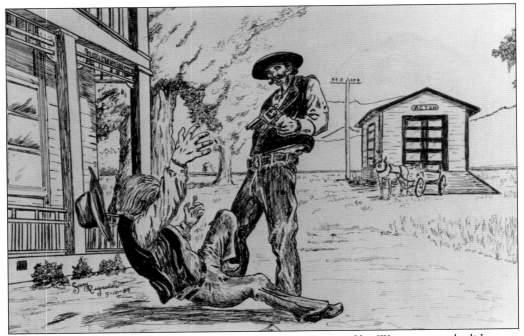

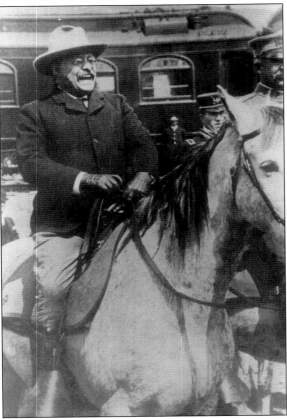

Despite film Westerns, rarely did combatants meet face-to-face in the street for a quick-draw duel—except in the Crown Valley Feud. It started with a years-long quarrel over a dog squabble between Acton's two leading citizens: German-born mayor D. M. Broom (no sense of humor) and the popular albeit deadly W. H. "Rosey" Melrose (practical joker). Rosey was faster. He hit Broom four times in the heart; the Los Angeles coroner's report later noted, "Good grouping." After two mistrials, Rosey was found innocent. Later Melrose would help nominate an Acton visitor and hunting pal to the Oval Office: Theodore (he hated "Teddy") Roosevelt. (Above courtesy Jerry Reynolds; below courtesy SCV Historical Society.)

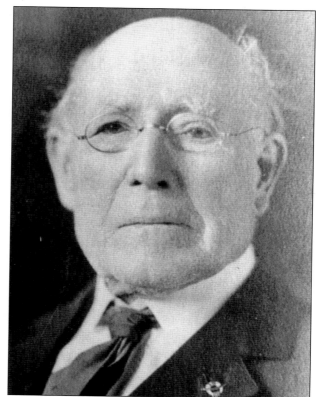

For 40 years, Judge John Powell reigned as the only law in the Santa Clarita Valley and never had a case overturned. Los Angeles County once asked if he would not mind paying for all his court costs out-of-pocket. John said "No." Powell was a famed big game hunter and still holds the record for bagging the largest mountain lion in California. The creature stretched 12 feet, 6 inches from nose to tip of tail. He also shot a rare white wolf in Bouquet Canyon. On his deathbed, he recalled the best deed of his life: meeting Dr. David Livingston in 1859. The pair freed 705 slaves from an African camp. Below is the judge in his front yard with family, in downtown Newhall, around 1903. (Both courtesy SCV Historical Society.)

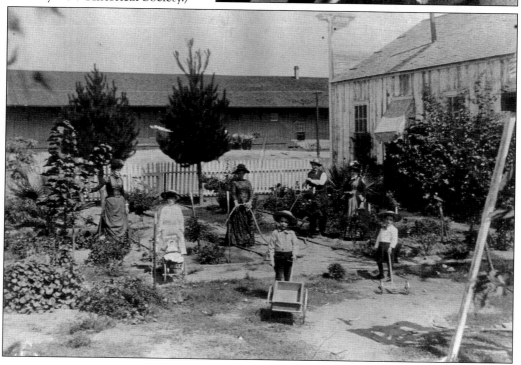

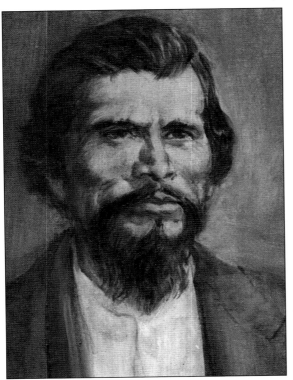

Womanizer, pistol fighter, murderer, and Hispanic Robin Hood, Tiburcio Vasquez was subject of the biggest manhunt in California history. His world-famous hideout, Vasquez Rocks, was named after him, as was a local high school. He was so bold that once, while chased by a posse, he stopped three times to rob people. When he was arrested in 1877, he was paraded through Los Angeles. Men stuffed bottles of brandy into his cage, and women gave him love letters. A playwright asked if Tiburcio could be let out of his cell so he could star as himself onstage. He owned three houses in the SCV and often posed as a horse trader, sometimes dining with leading citizens like Thomas Mitchell, John Lang, and even Judge Powell. He was hanged in San Jose for a murder after he and his gang had taken over the town of Tres Pinos. (Both courtesy SCV Historical Society.)

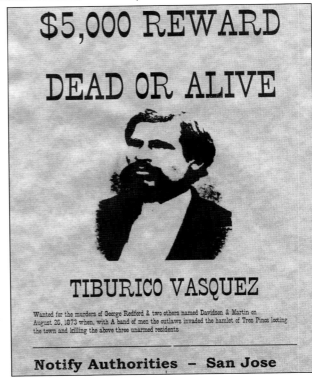

$5,000 REWARD

DEAD OR ALIVE

TIBURICO VASQUEZ

Wanted for the murders of George Redford & two others named Davidson & Martin on August 26, 1873 when, with A band of men the outlaws invaded the hamlet of Tres Pinos looting the town and killing the above three unarmed residents

Notify Authorities — San Jose

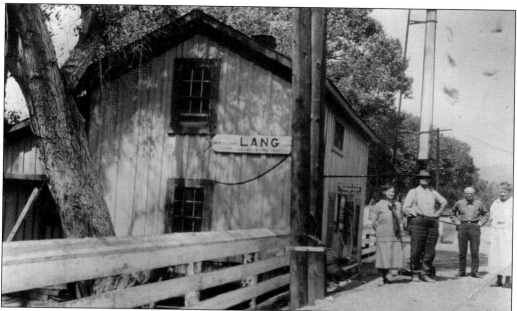

Today a gravel pit, Lang was once a posh resort, complete with hotel, eatery, and hot sulfur mineral springs to sooth the bone-weary traveler. Where the Rivers End resort is today, the resort was mudded up in the floods of 1938 and never reopened. It was named after rancher John Lang, who, despite owning 1,200 acres, did not own the land he sold to Southern Pacific. Lang had an impressive resume, which included building California's first cheese vats. Still a subject for heated debate today, Lang, in 1873, reportedly shot the world's largest grizzly, a monster that left a 19-inch-wide track, weighed 2,350 pounds, and reportedly swallowed six locals. Canyon Country today is a state historical landmark. (Both courtesy SCV Historical Society.)

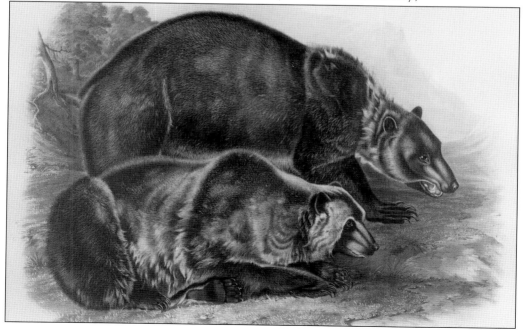

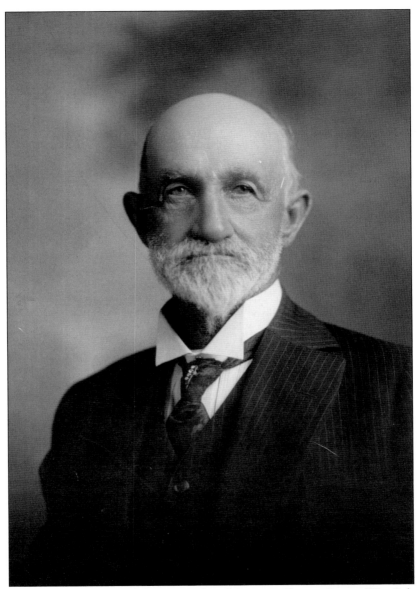

W. W. "Wert" Jenkins was one of the patriarchs of the great Castaic Range War. It lasted from 1876 to about 1916. Somewhere between 27 and 40 men (and one woman) were killed in one of the West's biggest land disputes. Called the Baron of Alcatraz (for attempting to homestead Alcatraz Island), Jenkins was sort of the Judge Roy Bean of Castaic. He carried at least double pistols, a rifle, and a brace of throwing knives. His nemesis was the equally tough and crusty William Chormicle. Chormicle's foreman, a man named Gardener, shot Jenkins point blank on Wert's porch. Three days later, Jenkins burned Gardener's house to the ground—with Gardener in it. One of Jenkins's sons, David, was lynched in nearby Bouquet Canyon, and for years, the area was called Hangman's Canyon or Dead Man's Canyon in honor of David. In 1905, Teddy Roosevelt appointed a special ranger to end the fighting. He did, for a while. Jenkins himself was shot several times, at close range, by Chormicle's men but ended up dying of old age. (Courtesy A. B. Perkins.)

Jenkins's nemesis, William Chormicle, had a tough childhood. While crossing the plains in a covered wagon, his parents were murdered by Native Americans, and W. C. was shot through the neck with an arrow. As an old man, Jenkins would live in a mountain cabin. He shot a 500-pound bear on his porch, which blocked the only door. Jenkins took three days to chisel out. His wife was Lavina. (Courtesy SCV Historical Society.)

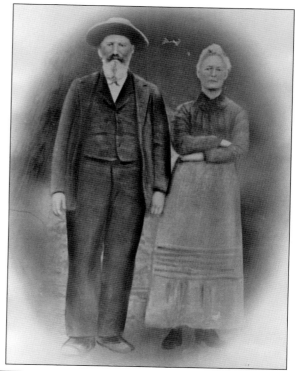

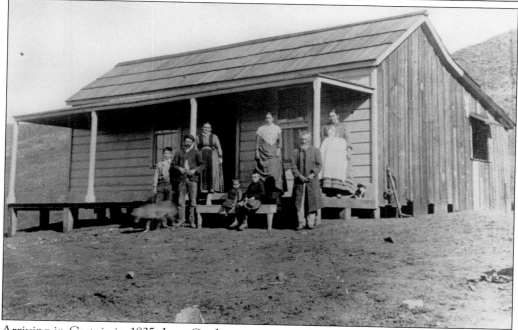

Arriving in Castaic in 1835, Juan Cordova was patriarch of one of the oldest families in the SCV. He served as a scout for John Fremont and founded a humble but large ranch. Many of the Cordova men were famous for being top cowhands, and many descendants still live in the SCV today. (Courtesy SCV Historical Society.)

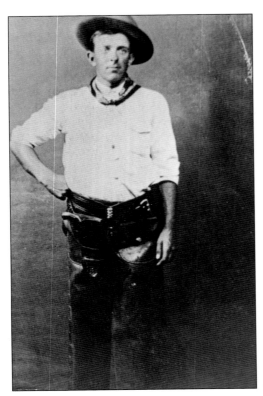

"Buffalo" Tom Vernon's parents were supposedly the Wyoming couple of Jim Averell and Ella Watson, also known as Cattle Kate. According to Vernon, at 11, he and his parents were kidnapped, and his parents were lynched by Carbon County cattle barons. Tom was saved by Chief Iron Tail, later the model for the Indian Head nickel. Vernon would later steal a cow from Saugus actor Harry Carey. (Courtesy SCV Historical Society.)

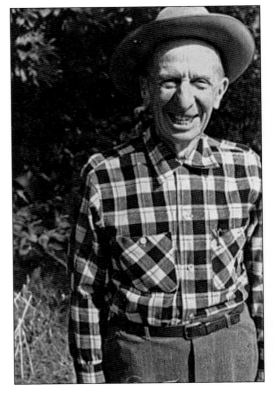

Before the "3 Strikes" law, Buffalo Tom had served five separate sentences in Folsom Prison. He was captured after dropping a detailed itinerary from his pocket. Before the law caught up him, he visited a prostitute in Wyoming and derailed and robbed another train. In prison, he wrote articles on horsemanship for national magazines. His life-in-prison sentence was commuted in 1957, and he lived with friends in Sacramento. (Courtesy Carolena Rezendes.)

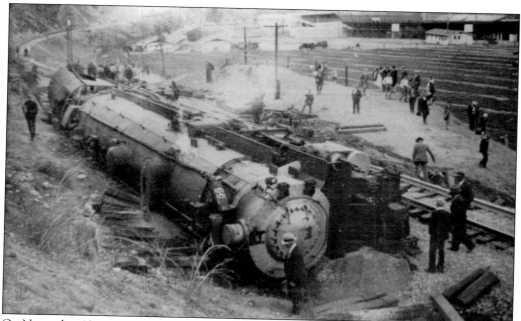

On November 10, 1929, "Buffalo" Tom Vernon (Tom Averell), a former rider in Buffalo Bill's Wild West Show, derailed the *West Coast Limited* at 7:45 behind today's Saugus Speedway. The engineer barely escaped being scalded to death, and Buffalo Tom liberated the passengers of about $300 in cash and small jewelry. During the manhunt, a man stumbled into the Newhall jail to confess. It turned out he was an escaped lunatic. Vernon later confessed that he needed the money for a "special operation" for a Hollywood madam. The Great Saugus Train Robbery was a short-lived boon to the local economy. Postcards were quickly printed. The train wreck site became a large tourist attraction for the next week as work crews labored to remove the monster engine and cars and rebuild Buffalo Tom's carnage. (Both courtesy Paul R. Ayers.)

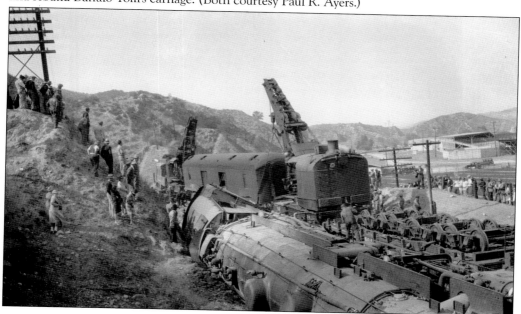

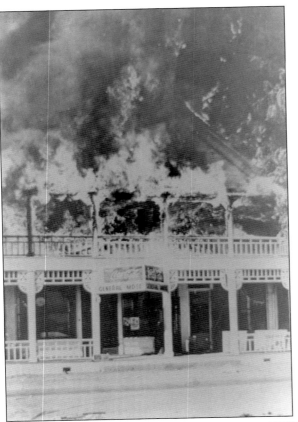

Acton Hotel owner Capt. Sam Schoor returned from World War II to find his best friend and one of Acton's leading citizens had swindled him out of thousands of dollars. When Schoor confronted his former best friend, the hotel manager Clarence Rush (who was also the postmaster), Rush threatened to burn down the historic inn if Captain Sam went to authorities. Sam did; Clarence torched the place. (Courtesy A. B. Perkins.)

Besides building one of the West's great inns, Rudolph Nickel was the publisher of the SCV's second newspaper: the *Acton Rooster*. (Billy Carlson's forgotten Newhall weekly newspaper from 1880 was the first). Nickel opened the lavish Acton Hotel in 1890. The Victorian-style resort welcomed many notables, including presidents Theodore Roosevelt, McKinley, Cleveland, and Hoover. Trains would take tourists to the famed Woodbine Resort up Aliso Canyon. (Courtesy A. B. Perkins.)

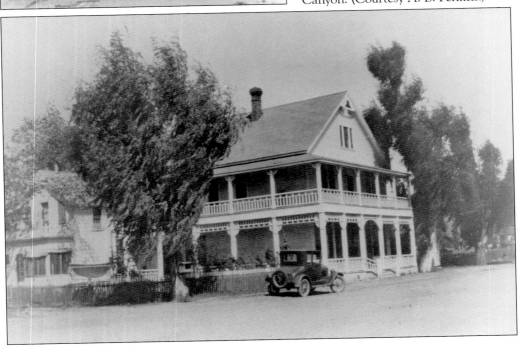

Four

EXCUSE ME.
DO YOU MINE?

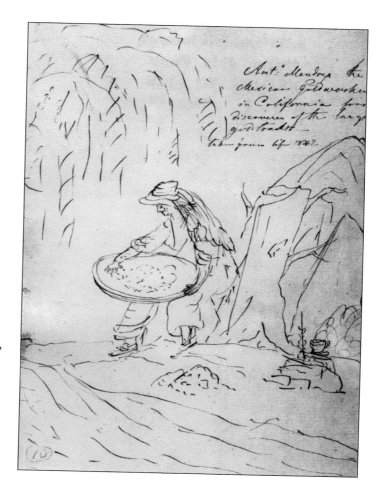

Miners from Mexico had a style of harvesting gold that required powerful lungs. Called "dry panning," the mineral hunter would take dirt in a straw basket, swirl, and blow. Try doing that for 10 hours. This sketch was from a Placerita Canyon miner's notebook from 1847. (Courtesy SCV Historical Society.)

NEW-YORK OBSERVER.

NEW-YORK, SATURDAY, OCTOBER 1, 1842.

SIDNEY E. MORSE & CO. EDITORS AND PROPRIETORS.

CALIFORNIA GOLD.—A letter from California, dated May 1, speaking of the discovery of gold in that country, says :— "They have at last discovered gold, not far from San Fernando, and gather pieces of the size of an eighth of a dollar. Those who are acquainted with these " placeres," as they call them, (for it is not a mine,) say it will grow richer, and may lead to a mine. Gold to the amount of some thousands of dollars has already been collected."

The Oak of the Golden Dream is the center of many debatable stories about the first major gold discovery in California. For years, many thought Sutter's Mill in Northern California was the site of the first gold find—in 1849. On his birthday, while hunting for onions for his wife's salad, Francisco Lopez and three forgotten friends started the Placerita strike in 1842. But 20 years earlier and a few miles across the valley, miners were pulling tons of ore from San Francisquito Canyon. Still earlier, in 1796, was the huge Lost Padre Mine in upper Castaic. Even the Oak of the Golden Dream has been questioned. Frank Hovore, former director of Placerita Canyon, shared a story that the original Oak of the Golden Dream burned down in a big fire and road crews just plunked a fresh sign at an untouched stately oak nearby and that the real Oak of the Golden Dream is actually on Walt Disney's property. Still, Placerita Canyon produced so much gold, including one 8-pound nugget, that it helped fuel the Gold Rush of 1849. (Courtesy SCV Historical Society.)

Francisco Lopez did all right for himself. For that 1842 first recorded gold discovery, the governor of California gave him the Rancho Temescal; then Lopez was given the Rancho Los Alamos. Old Spanish records indicate Lopez was joined by two friends on the claim, Manuel Cota and Domingo Bermudez, and a missing fourth person. Cota and Bermudez were the forgotten prospectors of SCV history. (Courtesy SCV Historical Society.)

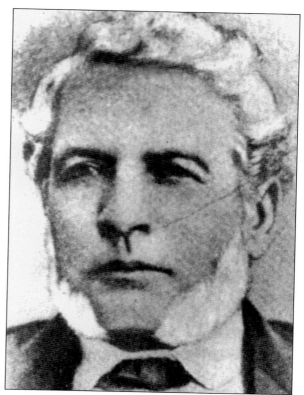

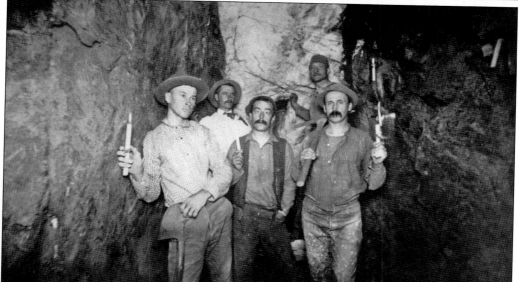

There are countless tales of SCV mining. The skeleton of an old prospector was once found in Haskell Canyon—with an oak growing out of his remains. In nearby Seco Canyon, the area was called Ratsburg around 1900 because gold hunters would scurry down shafts—like rats—when Newhall Land came to collect rent. Here miners mine the Red Rover. (Courtesy SCV Historical Society.)

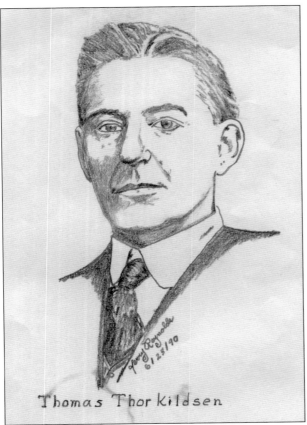

Thomas Thorkildsen

In 1908, at Davenport Road in Agua Dulce, Thomas Thorkidson bought a claim for $30,000 from two miners and formed the Sterling Borax Works. He built a narrow-gauge train line that hauled ore 6 miles over to Lang Station. Thorkidson lived a playboy's life, throwing lavish parties. A story was told that he was so proud of his physique, at a black-tie dinner, he stripped completely nude to show it to the ladies. He died, penniless, at 81 in a nursing home in La Crescenta in 1950. A small but thriving mining community with a school and stores named Sterling was founded and was operating into the 1920s. The mine played havoc on the environment. What also was left were hundreds of dead trees and thousands of plants choked to death from fine borax dust. (Both courtesy SCV Historical Society.)

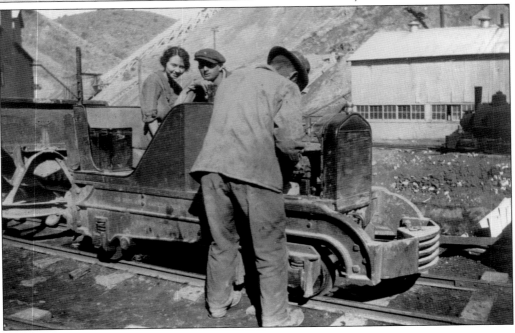

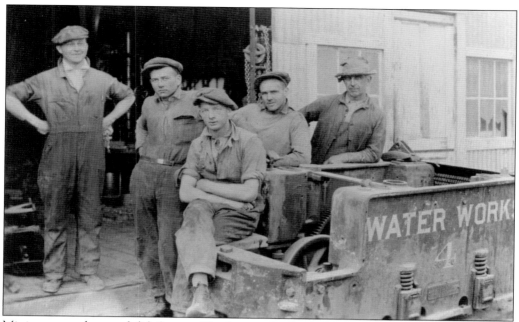

Mining was such a tough life for men like these at the Sterling Works and all over the valley, like Bouquet Canyon (below). Back in 1900, local miner Francisco Forjas turned up missing. Sixty-four years later, they found him—well, his skeleton. Local pioneer Annie Briggs identified some of the possessions found in a remote area between Tapia and Charlie Canyons. In 1967, sourdough Frank Pat Oliver, 62, was found in his little wooden cabin in upper Soledad. Right before he died, Frank scribbled down the name of his brother, who lived in New York City. The lonely prospector's body was found surrounded by his faithful pets: 15 cats, 30 chickens, 15 pigeons, a goat, and a dog. In 1934, a man dropped by the A. J. Bridger's B&Y Rancho, seeking some information on local gold mines. In conversation, the gent shared his résumé; he had worked for the following enterprises: Coffin Mine, Corpse Canyon, Funeral Range, and Death Valley. (Both courtesy SCV Historical Society.)

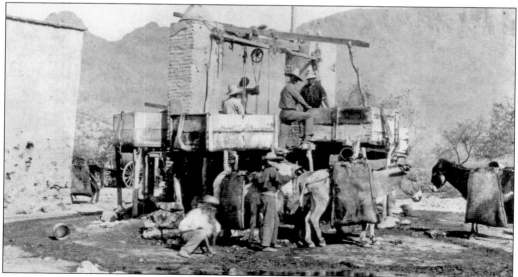

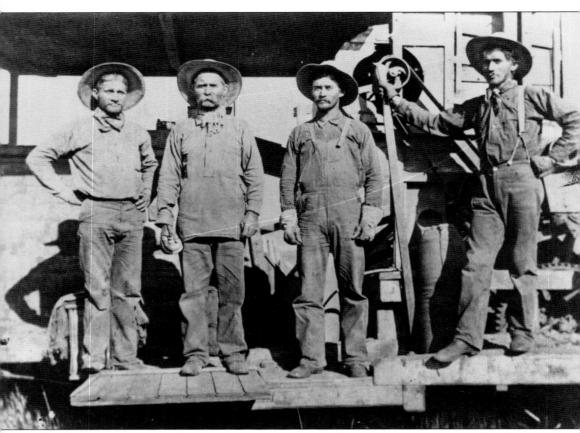

Much of the richness of the SCV comes from an epic flood millions of years ago that deposited countless tons of various ore and minerals. During the Civil War, beautiful copper ingots, shaped like leaves and lined with silver, were being pulled out in the hills from modern Canyon Country up to Acton. Huge wagon convoys carrying gold, silver, copper, and quartz rumbled out of the valley to Oxnard and then up mostly to San Francisco. A Los Angeles newspaper suggested creating a big tunnel from the San Fernando Valley to Newhall so the ore would not be lost to the Buenaventura area. Scruffy miners were selling their claims for anywhere from $20,000 to a quarter million to San Francisco businessmen and speculators. The hearty souls above were photographed in Pico Canyon. (Courtesy SCV Historical Society.)

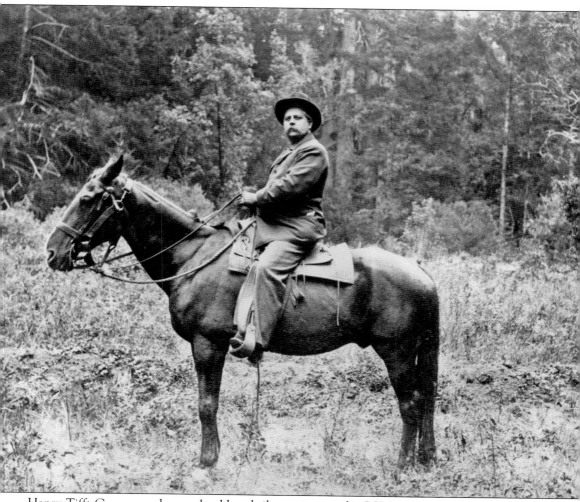

Henry Tifft Gage owned several gold and silver mines in the SCV, most of them in the Agua Dulce/Acton area. Few realize he also owned a gold mine that now sits submerged beneath the Bouquet Reservoir. Horseman, rancher, sheepherder, and millionaire, he was governor of California from 1899 to 1903. About 30 years later, the new mine owner, Samuel Tate, put 20 men to work at the old Governor Gage (the "Red Rover") mine. The Sierra Pelona pit was nicknamed Rip Van Winkle because people would come in, take out a few million bucks in gold and quartz, and then the vein would disappear for years, only to "wake" again. (Courtesy SCV Historical Society.)

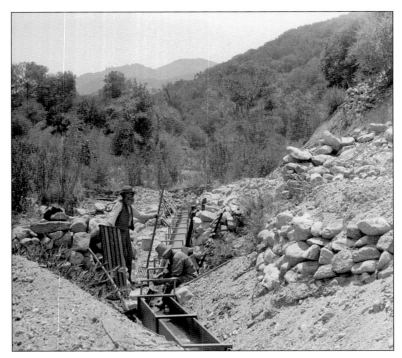

Re-enactors show how miners laid claim to upper Placerita Canyon in the 1840s. Gold fever hit in the 1930s, easing the Depression locally. With the St. Francis Dam washing away topsoil through the ore-rich valley, thousands of prospectors looked for the next mother lode. It was also a boon to local businessmen, who sold everything from pans to sack lunches and "How To Pan For Gold" books. (Courtesy SCV Historical Society.)

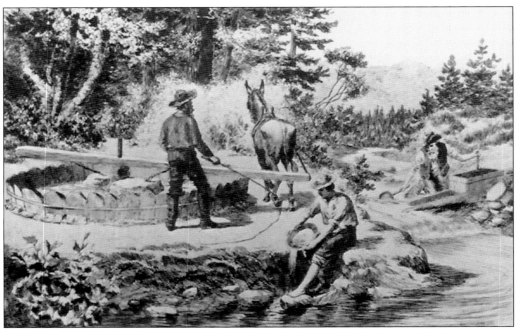

There are many fables of lost mines in the SCV. In 1921, a forest ranger found a huge vein in upper Placerita Canyon assaying out at $1,700 a ton. He also found a ledge of gold, a yard thick, sticking out of a mountain. He planned to retire and come back for the treasure but died a few months later, taking the location with him. This quartz-crushing arrastra is like the one in Sand Canyon. (Courtesy SCV Historical Society.)

Five

OIL'S WELL
THAT ENDS WELL

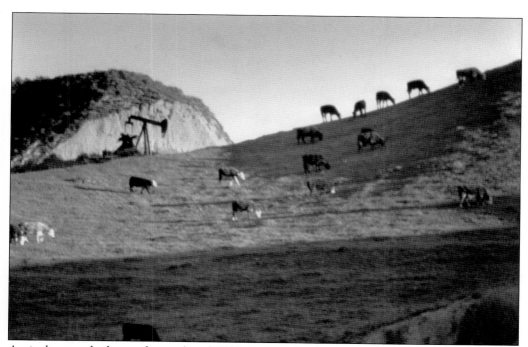

Agriculture and oil were the staples of SCV economy for decades. In 1893, Newhall Land owned 400 horses and 2,000 head of cattle and harvested everything from oranges to wheat. In Placerita Canyon, in the 1870s, some of earth's purest oil—clear and 100 times purer than regular crude—was bubbling out of the ground. That open well is still there in Placerita, at a secret location. (Courtesy SCV Historical Society.)

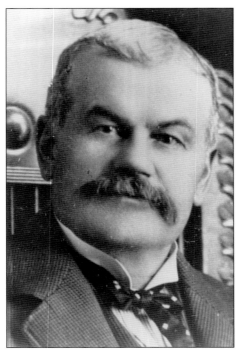

Pico No. 4 was an amazing oil well, the first commercially successful one in the West. From its first barrel in 1876, it continued pumping until 1990—making it the longest running well in the world. Using California's first steam-driven oil rig, Alex Mentry improved an existing well from the 1860s. By 1880, he had turned a lonely canyon into a boomtown called, appropriately, Mentryville, housing more than 100 families and more single men. A schoolhouse, which is still there today, was erected in 1885. In 1888, Mentry and his family moved into a 13-room mansion, which was recently restored after the 1994 Northridge Quake. Mentry died in 1900, victim of the assassin bug, also called the kissing bug, a venomous insect. (Both courtesy Santa Monica Mountains Conservancy; donated by Chevron USA.)

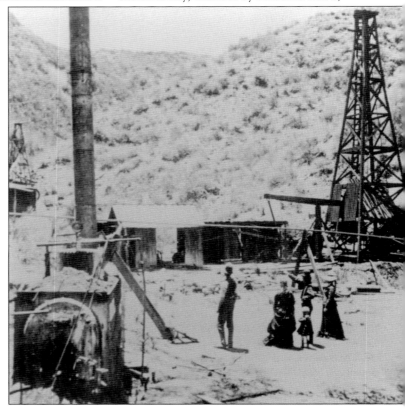

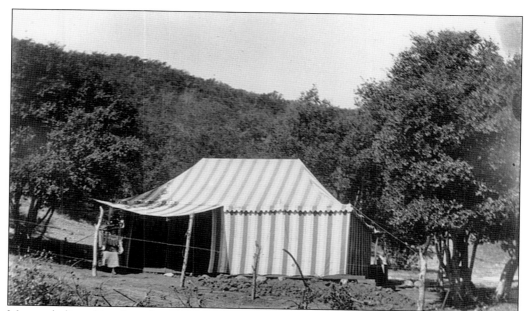

Mentry believed in clean living and forbade his men to swear. (The single ones usually lived in tents, like the one here in Pico Canyon.) He kept a large "Swear Jar" handy to collect fines. Mentryville operated during the height of Prohibition, so there was not any drinking either, except the amounts smuggled in on the daily stage. (Courtesy SCV Historical Society.)

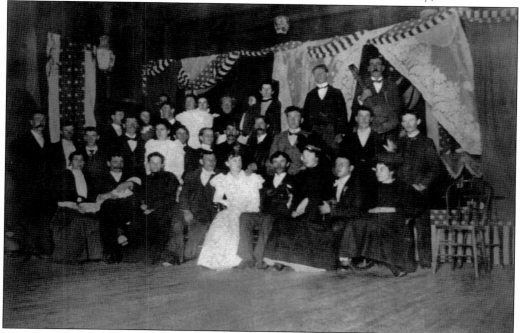

Mentryville was a charming, self-sufficient community nestled in Pico Canyon. It had a lighted (natural gas) tennis court and a dance hall. The place has a reputation for being haunted, and in the 1940s, according to *Signal* editor Fred Trueblood, there were Bigfoot sightings there. Today, like many of the historically rich sights, it is a state historical area. (Courtesy SCV Historical Society.)

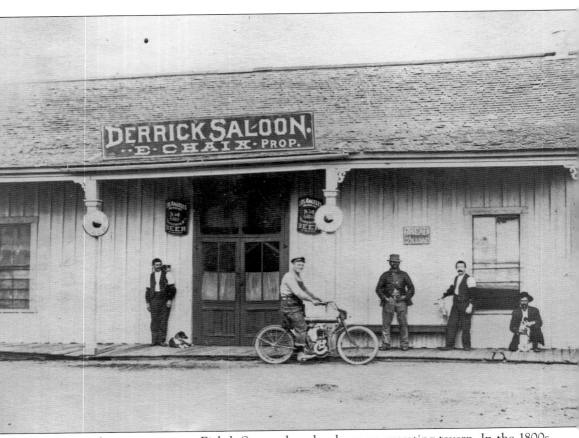

For more than a century, on Eighth Street, there has been an operating tavern. In the 1800s, it was the Derrick, attracting primarily oil workers. Today the place is called the Rendezvous. One of the more infamous oilmen of the SCV was Milfred Yant. In the 1930s, he went to San Quentin prison for conning seniors in a complicated oil scam. Broke, he tried it again in the 1940s, only to find the lower Placerita property he owned was actually sitting on an underground sea of petroleum. Eventually, he and a silent partner would see 150 wells pull out 18 million barrels, disrupting the price of world crude. (Courtesy SCV Historical Society.)

Six

THE NAVEL
OF THE UNIVERSE

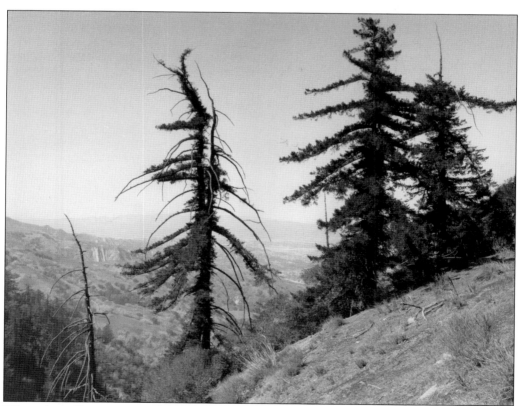

When the valley was covered with hundreds of thousands of spruce (seen here) and, later, oak, the concept of getting stuck in traffic was not of much importance to the people living here. The Native Americans did not have pianos or oil barrels to move. But the Santa Clarita Valley was a natural barrier for people eager to be elsewhere. (Courtesy SCV Historical Society.)

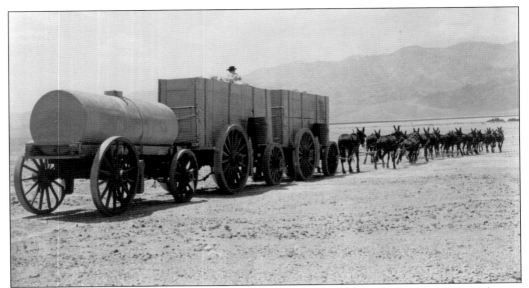

By the early 19th century, it became important to move things efficiently. The through roads were terrible. It took a woman of means seven days to travel from Camulos to downtown Los Angeles—usually by oxcart—via Ventura, crossing the creek dozens of times. As the mining interest boomed, it became more important to have wide working roads. (Courtesy SCV Historical Society.)

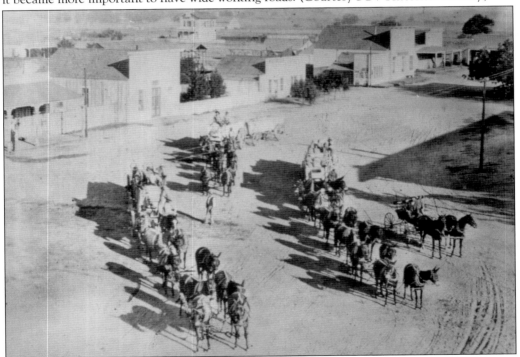

This is downtown Newhall in 1889 at the peak of traffic gridlock. Prior to 1863, one could not even think of driving a wagon to the San Fernando Valley. There were major gold strikes going on everywhere, and merchants in Los Angeles could not reach them to deliver much-needed supplies. (Courtesy SCV Historical Society.)

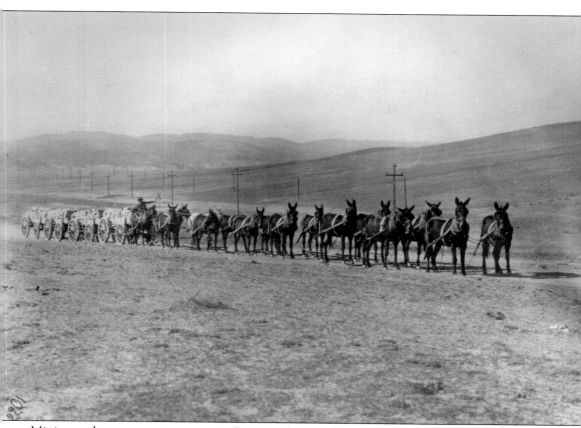

Mining and transportation magnate Remi Nadeau used to run convoys of huge 20-plus mule teams through the SCV in the 19th century. Nadeau noticed that from the rich Mojave mines, it was a straight line through Saugus on to Oxnard/Ventura. Nadeau wanted to make Oxnard/Ventura the Southland's major city instead of Los Angeles. A teamster named Three-Toed Pete used to navigate mule teams as long as 60 creatures. The SCV is famous for its legacy of gold, copper, and silver mines. But it also has one of earth's largest stashes of graphite and titanium. Unfortunately for the latter, it is buried under the tony Beverly Hills district of Sand Canyon real estate. (Courtesy SCV Historical Society.)

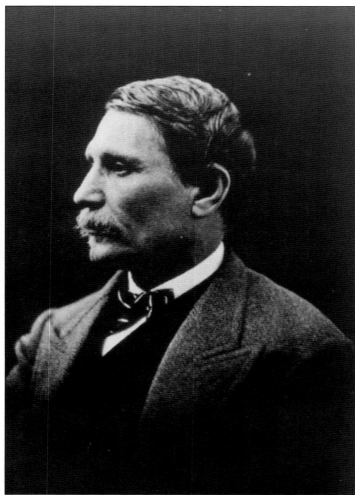

The controversial Gen. Edward Fitzgerald Beale used his various government connections to make a fortune in real estate, only to lose it all by trying to corner the sheep market in Los Angeles. Around 1863, Beale was paid to finish what would eventually be a 90-foot slice in a mountain that today is a state historic location: Beale's Cut. Beale not only used U.S. Cavalry troops to complete the project for free; for 21 years, he charged a toll on anything with legs or wheels passing through. Before the Civil War, Beale convinced U.S. Secretary of War Jefferson Davis to petition Congress to invest in camels to explore parts of the SCV and beyond. A colorful parade of the beasts passed through the SCV in 1858 to a rousing 100-gun salute. (Both courtesy SCV Historical Society.)

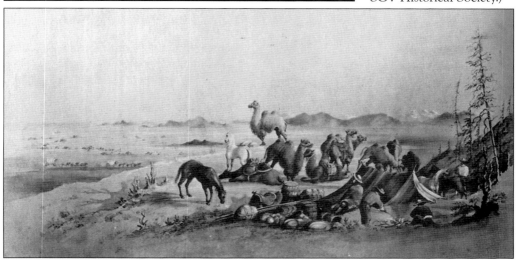

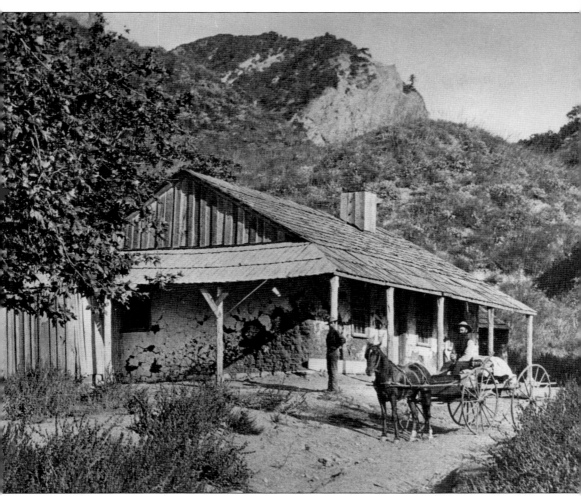

Beale's tollhouse was not famous for its cookies. After keepers A. A. Hudson and Oliver Robbins started it in partnership with Beale, the Dunn family ran it. (Beale kept two-thirds of every toll, ranging from 3¢ per sheep to $2 for large wagons.) In 1875, a sheepherder found a Mrs. Dunn alone at the gate. He refused to pay a woman and stampeded his small flock through. Mrs. Dunn armored up, trailed him to the San Fernando Valley, and waited for nightfall. She woke him with a shotgun to the nose and demanded "$16.25—$2.75 for the toll and the balance for the gatekeeper's injured feelings." He paid. (Courtesy SCV Historical Society.)

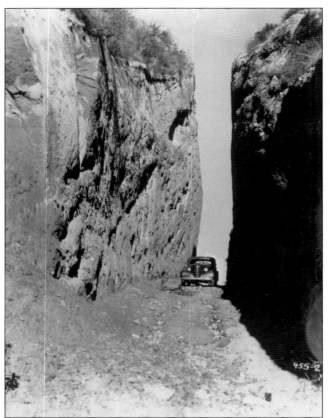

Remember that Phineas Banning started a road east of the pre–Beale's Cut. Early cars had a tough time locomoting up Beale's Cut. The first vehicle over the top was a 1902 Autocar. It had to drive in reverse because the gravity-based carburetor kept stalling. Bob Walk, grandfather of World Series pitcher Bob Walk IV, made a nice side living towing cars over the grade with his mules. (Courtesy SCV Historical Society.)

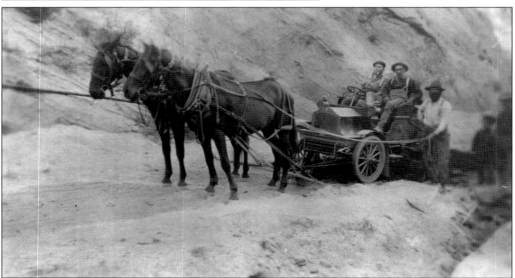

Motorists in the early 20th century had to contend with rockslides, potholes, and transmission-ending boulders, but at least they did not have to face grizzlies, as did early stage riders. The bruins would stop traffic by scratching their backs on telegraph poles alongside the road. The beasts thought the humming sound from the wires came from bees. (Courtesy SCV Historical Society.)

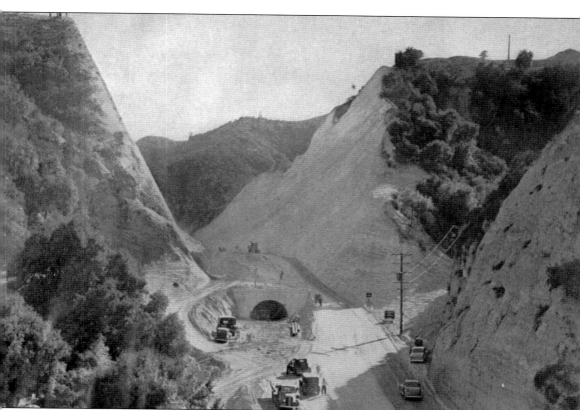

From 1910 to 1938, the main road into the valley from the San Fernando side was via the Newhall road tunnel. It's under present-day Sierra Highway—next to Beale's Cut. They filled in and cut the current Sierra Highway grade just south of town. Note how much mountain was removed and imagine driving a car over that. The tunnel removal project cost $100,000. In the 1920s, a 50-ton boulder that was perched above the south entrance fell, nearly killing a couple and a state police officer on motorcycle. The avalanche caused an explosion of air, shooting the biker out the other end like a bullet. In 1924, the paving of roads was still more of a crafts project than science. The main highway out of the Newhall Tunnel had an ongoing problem: it would not exactly melt, but it would soften on hot days. Adding to the cartoon aspect of the road, as it softened under heavy traffic, when someone hit the brakes, the road would curl up like a ribbon. Locals likened it to "driving over a giant washboard." (Courtesy SCV Historical Society.)

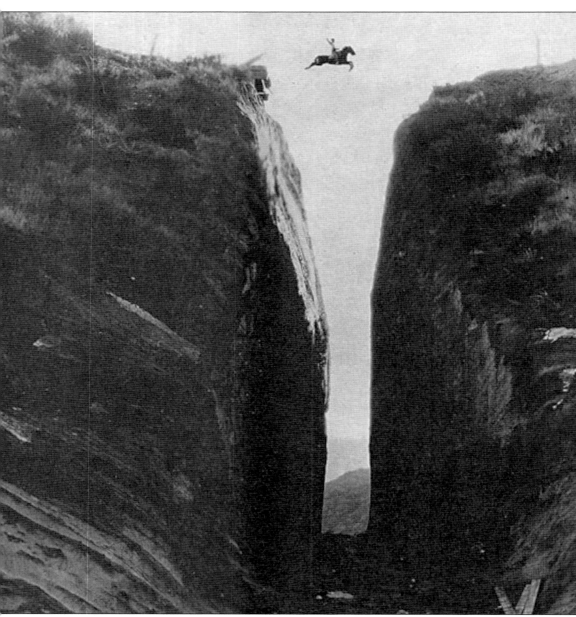

In its day, this was one of the most talked-about stunts in America. Fox Films publicity made Tom Mix take credit for this "jump" over Beale's Cut on the south end of Newhall. Actually, Mix and his wonder horse, Tony (who is reportedly buried somewhere under Veteran's Park on Newhall Avenue), rode across a wooden bridge, and the special effect was spliced in for John Ford's 1923 film *Three Jumps Ahead*. Placerita's Andy Jauregui reportedly made the jump, as did supposedly another stuntman. Another rumor noted that one stuntman died in an attempt. Will Rogers later "duplicated" the mighty leap. Kidding his friend Mix, Rogers and his horse Soapdish, in mid-air, performed a triple somersault. Audiences howled. (Courtesy Leon Worden.)

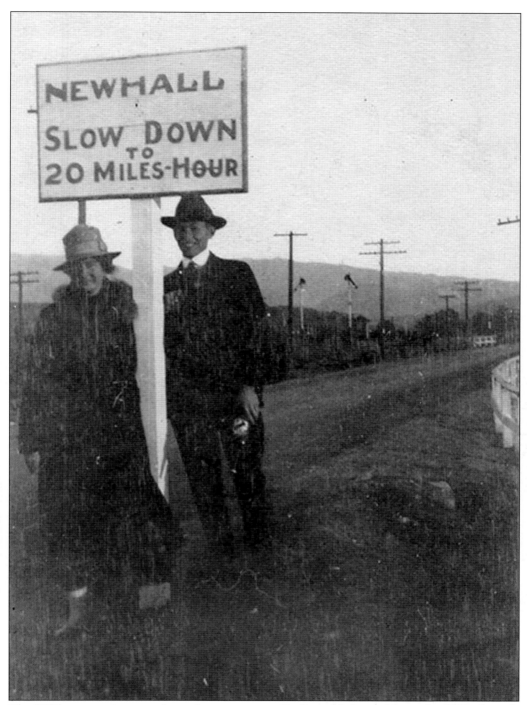

The SCV was a serious speed trap for many years. On State Highway 6 from the 1920s through 1950s, lawmen used creative means to distribute tickets. The state police would stop motorists at Castaic and write up a code time on a slip of paper. If the motorist made it to the other end of the valley too early, they were ticketed for speeding. (Courtesy SCV Historical Society.)

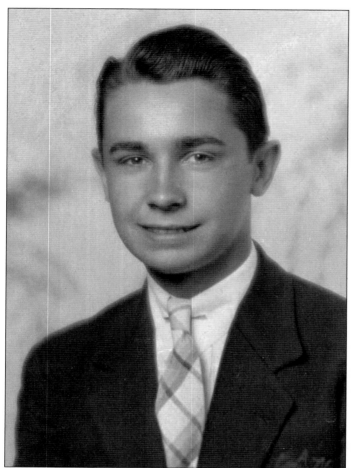

Gene Doty was 10 years old in the 1930s when he was the manager of Newhall's grocery store. In high school, he was the lessee of the Shell Gas Station (which had a reputation for the cleanest restrooms in the state). He founded the Newhall Tennis Club in 1948, and sneaking up on 90 in 2008, Gene still plays and runs a tennis company. His father, Jesse Doty, opened the Ford Garage in the early 20th century. In 1916, Jesse used to attract customers by hiring the two prettiest girls in town. In bathing suits (from ankles to chins), they would wave at motorists to come in for a fill-up. Back then, gas was a dime a gallon and poured, with ladles, from wooden barrels. A giant sign in the garage greeted customers: "Absolutely No Credit." (Both courtesy Genene Triepuhtrohl-Staats.)

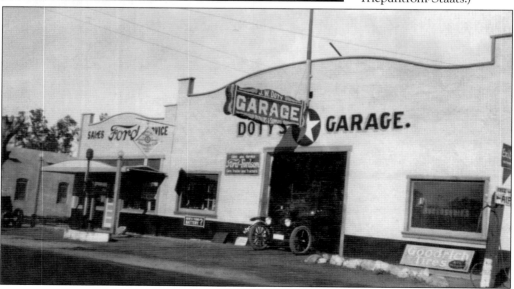

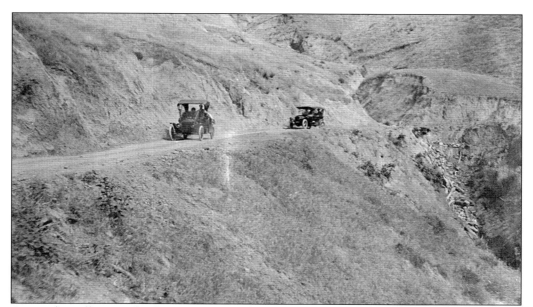

Across the valley was the Grapevine, named after the old Spanish trail lined with wild grapes. Kit Carson and Grizzly Adams hiked through the original trail (which was 15 miles east). In 1912, in a statewide move to link and improve SCV roads, California began State Highway 4. The Ridge Route opened in 1915 as a two-lane concrete highway and cost $3 million to build. (Courtesy Leon Worden.)

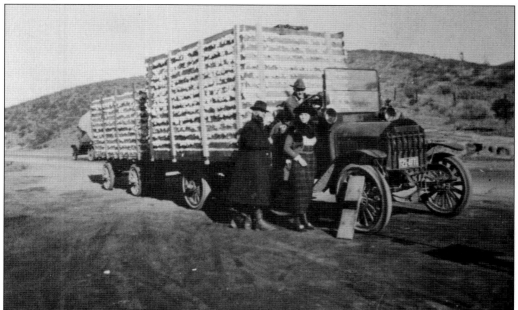

Because of its tortuous grades and curves (942 between Castaic and the San Joaquin Valley), the Ridge Route was a nightmare for truckers and those behind them. While most big rigs were made back East, nearly every truck-maker in America tested their vehicles on the Ridge Route. Why? It had the worst conditions in the country. What was the top speed for uphill trucks in 1915? Try 2 miles per hour. (Courtesy SCV Historical Society.)

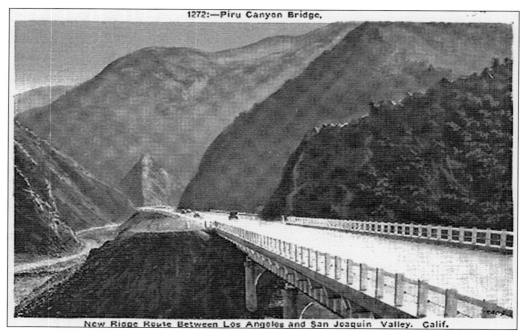

1272:—Piru Canyon Bridge.

New Ridge Route Between Los Angeles and San Joaquin Valley. Calif.

There were many deaths and accidents on the old Ridge Route. In 1915, *Fortnight Magazine* noted, "People who made the journey wrote adventure books about it." Bandits sometimes jumped on running boards at hairpin curves and held up travelers. According to the *Signal*, twice the drivers sped up and rammed the robbers into boulders. (Courtesy Leon Worden.)

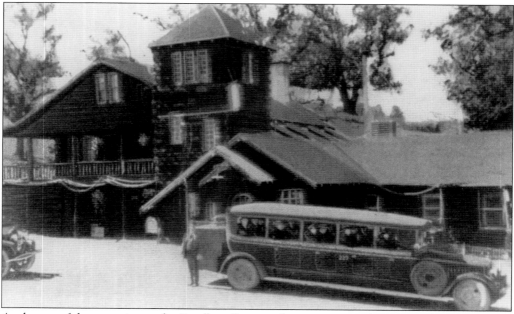

At the top of the summit was the Sandberg Resort, where weary travelers, nature lovers, hunters, and even murders visited. Richard John Jensen, the SCV's only known serial killer, plied his grisly trade along the Ridge Route and was sentenced to death in a Newhall Court in 1956. Other than that, the Sandberg was a great place to stay. (Courtesy SCV Historical Society.)

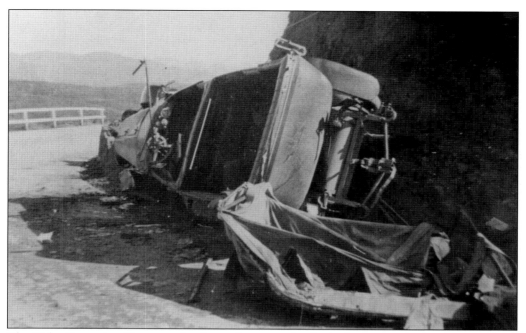

The Ridge Route is still open today (sort of; one needs a high-clearance vehicle and must make sure the road is not washed out). Tourists can see sheer drop-offs, some nearly 1,000 feet, and the ruins of old gas stations, eateries, and vistas. The Grapevine Café rested at the base of a steep hill, dangerously close to the road. It was wiped out five times by runaway trucks before the owners finally abandoned it. (SCV Historical Society.)

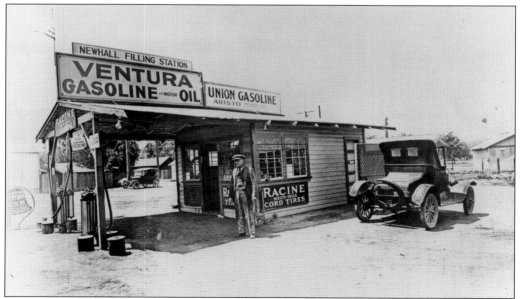

Carl Sischo opened the Newhall Filling Station, the first gas station in the valley, in 1917 (the photograph is from 1926) at the corner of Eighth Street and the current Main Street. Gasoline was delivered in big wooden barrels on a wagon pulled by a team of horses. Gas cost about a dime a gallon and was under 30¢ until the early 1970s. (Courtesy SCV Historical Society.)

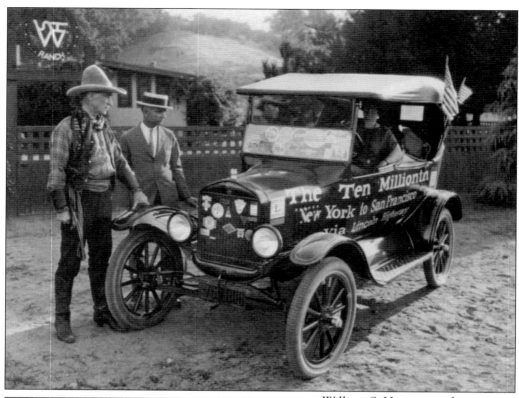

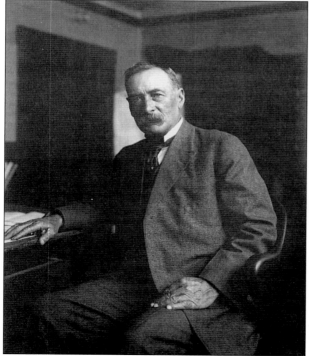

William S. Hart greets the 10-millionth Ford produced on its U.S. tour in the 1920s. Local Ford dealer Jesse Doty employed a salesman who had a special trick. He would take customers on a test drive to steep Beale's Cut. The car hawker would bring a camera and beverages, stopping a few times up the grade to take pictures. That way, the car would not overheat. (Courtesy SCV Historical Society.)

William Mulholland designed the California Aqueduct from the Owens Valley and the ill-fated St. Francis Dam. Mulholland Drive was named after the engineer. In the 1920s, the state planned to bring the road into the SCV through a tiny forgotten dirt road that is still on the maps today: Saugus to the Sea. The Depression stopped that link. (Courtesy SCV Historical Society.)

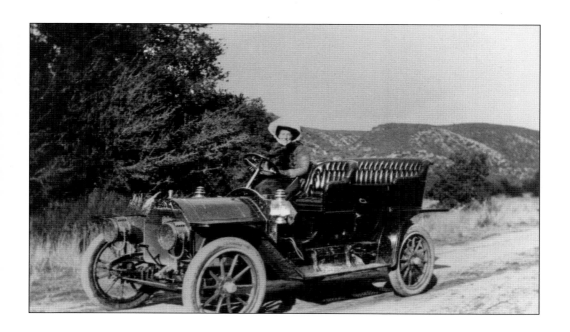

Wallace Hardison and Lyman Stewart owned this oil storage building (below), but the partners were not too adept at their business. They drilled a series of dry wells near Pico Canyon and fell onto hard times. So they left town and started Union Oil in Santa Paula. That company did a little better. Later, Frances Phillips bought the place and turned it into a boardinghouse. Phillips is famous for buying the first car (above) in the SCV—a 1906 Cadillac. That stately oak in front of the building was called the Hanging Tree and was across from Campton's General Store. Not only were criminals sometimes chained to it, some were hanged from the branches as well. (Both courtesy SCV Historical Society.)

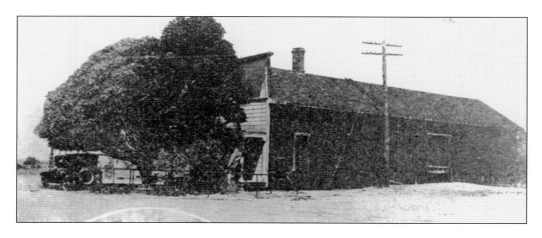

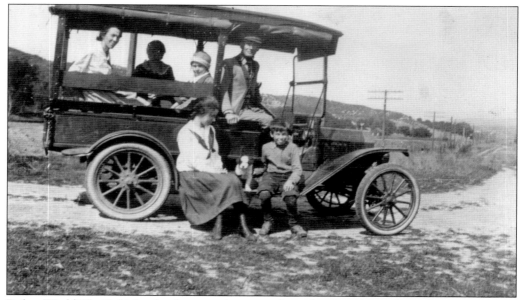

Before World War II, high school–age students were bussed to San Fernando High. In 1918, David Dill turned his pickup into a school bus. Kids bounced 30-plus miles or longer. Dill improved the ride by putting on a canvas top for when it rained and adding wooden benches. Many kids were away from home 13 hours because of the commute. (Courtesy SCV Historical Society.)

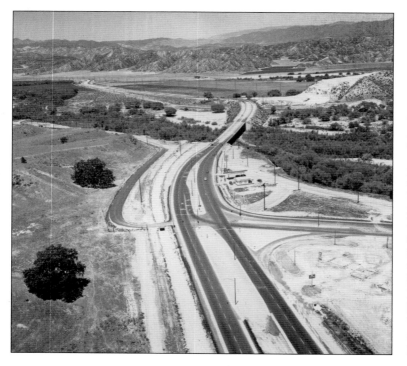

This is a late-1960s photograph of a brand-new Interstate 5 going through Newhall. Earlier in 1954, maps of a new "Golden State Freeway" were shown in the *Signal* newspaper, along with the amusing headline: "Gigantic Hiway Project To End Traffic Jams." Well, not yet. (Courtesy SCV Historical Society.)

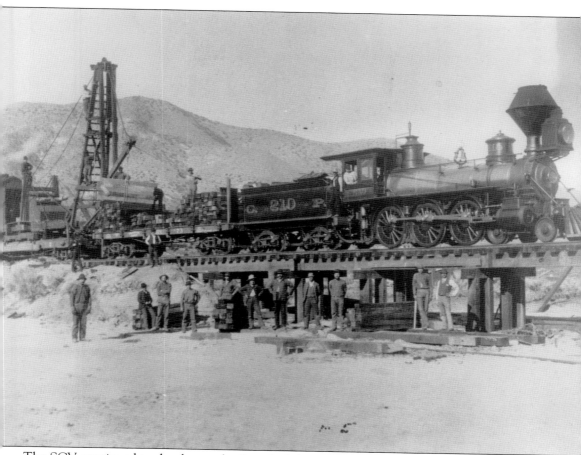

The SCV continued to develop as the "navel of the universe" in the 19th century. As roads continued to improve, a new medium of transportation invaded the SCV: the train. With a blast of Hercules dynamite in 1875, work began on building the fourth-largest railroad tunnel in the world. Working from the San Fernando and SCV sides, the 7,000-foot-tunnel was completed July 14, 1876. In an amazing feat of engineering, the tunnel was off by only one-half inch. It linked Northern and Southern California, and the new town of Newhall would be in the catbird seat. Interestingly, the topper to all transportation plans was unveiled after World War II. The state planned a 26-mile tunnel from Castaic to the San Joaquin Valley. On the bottom tier would be train tracks, in the middle a road for trucks, and, on top, a road for cars. This great rabbit hole was never built—so far. (Courtesy SCV Historical Society.)

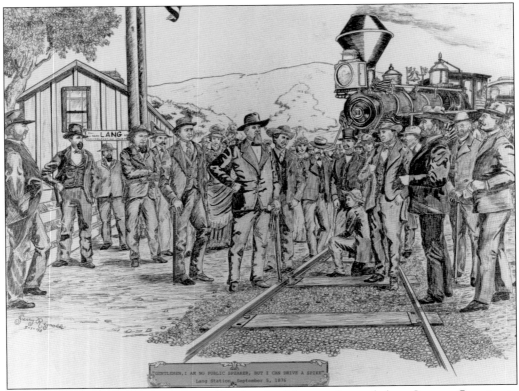

"GENTLEMEN, I AM NO PUBLIC SPEAKER, BUT I CAN DRIVE A SPIKE"
Lang Station, September 5, 1876

On September 5, 1876, a contingent of land and rail barons descended on Canyon Country to link the east and west by rail. As Leland Stanford, Colis Huntington, and about 1,500 Chinese laborers in new denim outfits watched, the golden spike was driven by Charles Crocker in six hits. One dignitary quipped that Lang was "fit only for the production of horned toads and scorpions." The town of Newhall was founded the same day—where Saugus sits today. Every board of the original Newhall depot (below) was moved to where the Metrolink sits today on Market Street. The old Newhall train depot was abandoned in the 1930s to save money, turned into a potato packing shed, and burned in the 1960s. Originally, there were 11 rail tunnels in the SCV. Most were blown up during World War II to deter terrorists. (Courtesy SCV Historical Society.)

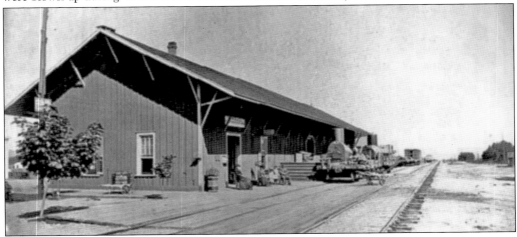

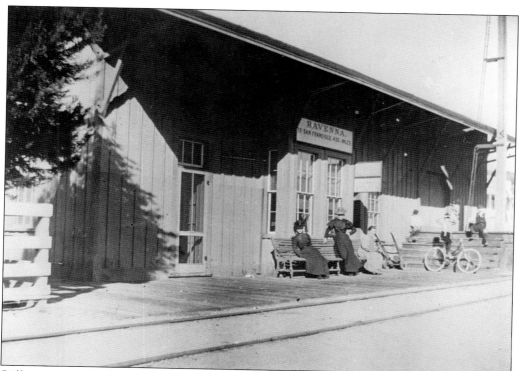

Still on many maps but long forgotten by most is the community of Ravenna. It's located about halfway between Acton and Agua Dulce and, in its heyday, was a booming mining community complete with its own rail stop. It was called Soledad City. Because of another Soledad up north, the U.S. postmaster renamed it after a grocer strolling past, Manuel Ravenna. (Courtesy SCV Historical Society.)

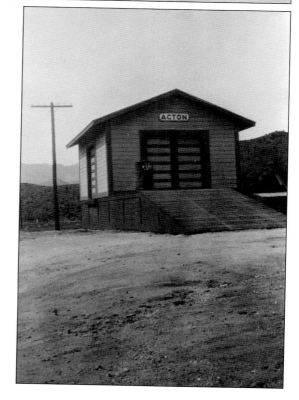

It's hard to believe that Acton, named after a town in Massachusetts, was considered as a site for California's capital. Up the road from Lang, Acton was a major boomtown. This train depot burned to the ground in June 1927. (Courtesy SCV Historical Society.)

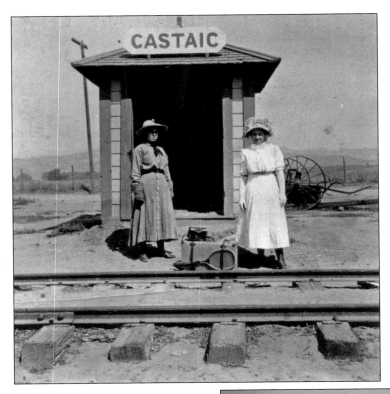

Notice that the sign for the Castaic Train Depot (built in 1887) is almost as large as the depot. A post office opened in 1894 and closed a year later. No one was sending mail. No one was receiving any. May MacDonald and Ethel Casey wait for the next train in this 1909 photograph. The station was wiped out in the St. Francis Dam disaster. (Courtesy SCV Historical Society.)

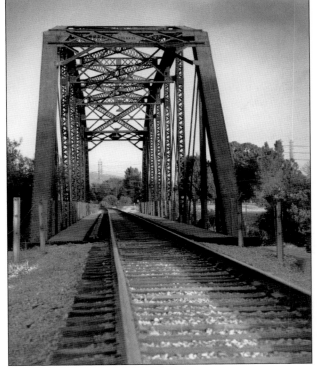

Rebuilt after the 1928 St. Francis Dam disaster and hauled in, this Southern Pacific bridge is still next to Farmer Nancy's Christmas Tree Farm on Magic Mountain Parkway and was a link from Newhall to Santa Barbara and beyond. Talk around city hall and Newhall Land is that maybe, someday, they will reconnect the SCV to the ocean via rail. (Courtesy SCV Historical Society.)

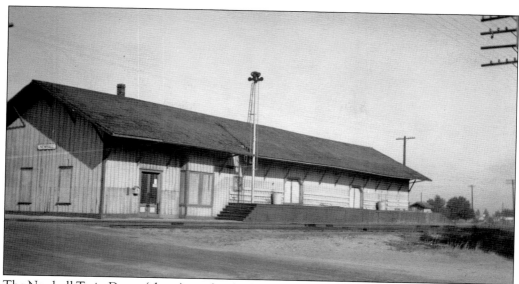

The Newhall Train Depot (above) was first built in 1876 in what is today Saugus. In 1876, Saugus was called Newhall. Every board of the depot, plus the rest of the town of Newhall, moved 2 miles south in 1878. In 1888, the Saugus Depot (below) was built atop the Newhall Depot's same foundation—the same day the Castaic Depot opened. The Newhall Depot closed in 1933 because it just was not making money. It became a potato-packing shed and burned down in 1960 on a night so cold the fire hydrants froze. In 1953, Leah Rosenfeld was the new Saugus agent. She and her husband, the agent at the San Joaquin station, had 23 children. They would put two or three on a train, establish wire confirmation, and exchange them. (Both courtesy SCV Historical Society.)

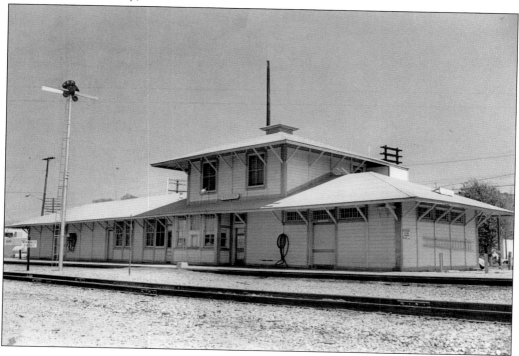

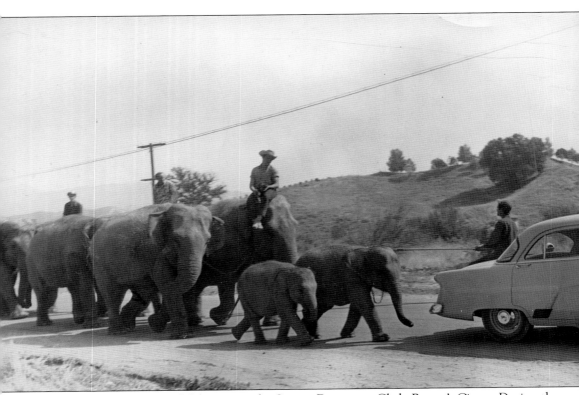

One of the most unusual deliveries at the Saugus Depot was Clyde Beatty's Circus. During the 1950s, the valley was the winter home to Beatty's traveling show. Elephants would literally march from the Saugus Train Station, down Lyons Avenue, to where Del Prado's condos are today. Beatty would bed down his big tent, and the roar of lions and tigers would wake up chickens and humans alike. One of the more unusual crimes at the Saugus Depot happened in the early 1920s. Thirsty crooks crawled under a freight loaded with barrels of sacramental wine bound for the Los Angeles Archdiocese. Using huge augers, wine liberators drilled through the floor and emptied several casks, filling up their own barrels in the ditch by the tracks. (Courtesy SCV Historical Society.)

Seven

MULHOLLAND'S FOLLY

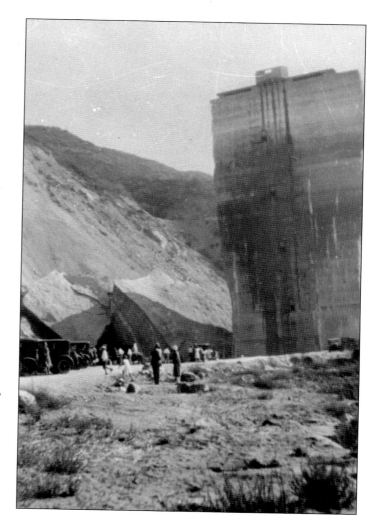

Next to the San Francisco earthquake and fire, the St. Francis Dam disaster was the worst disaster in California history. When the face of the dam gave way shortly before midnight, March 12, 1928, a nearly 200-foot-tall wall of water washed everything from top soil and livestock to trees and 100-ton boulders down San Francisquito Canyon. Nearly 500 died. (Courtesy SCV Historical Society.)

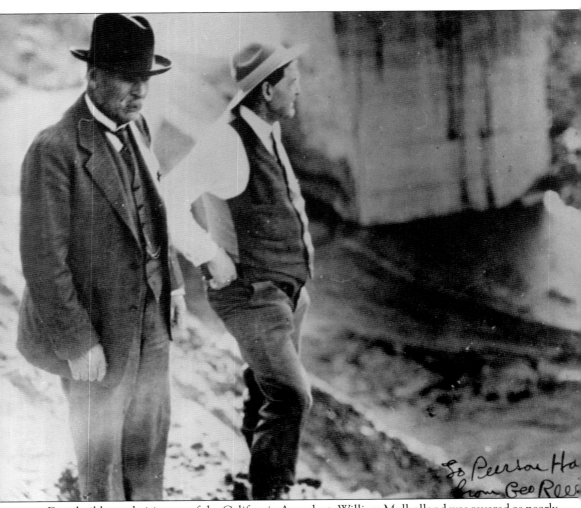

To Peerion Ha
from Geo Ree

Dam builder and visionary of the California Aqueduct, William Mulholland was revered as nearly a god. Reports in the *Signal* newspaper prior to 1928 told of locals—including rural postman W. Stonecypher, who refused to go up the canyon—warning Mulholland that geology in San Francisquito Canyon was unstable. Some locals wanted Mulholland tried for murder. Decades later, scientists confirmed that the dam was built against an ancient earthquake fault line. In 1913, up Hauser Canyon off Mint Canyon near the Sierra Highway, Mulholland bought 300 acres and set up a model farm that grew hybrid grains. He apparently built an epic house of "native rock and city cement." When he died in 1935, the estate was sold to the Lannan family. It was decaying as of 1979. Harvey Van Norman (right) is shown inspecting the St. Francis catastrophe the morning after. (Courtesy SCV Historical Society.)

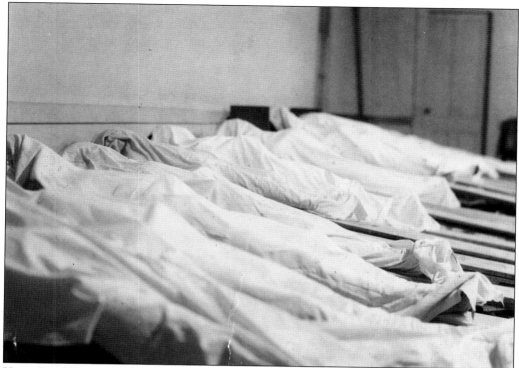

Hap-a-Land Dance Hall was the valley's social soul, hosting dances, parties, silent movies, and meetings. It was turned into a morgue to house victims of the St. Francis disaster. People did not want to go in after that, and it was torn down. The building was replaced by the courthouse in 1932 on Market Street. The original oak dance floor today sits upstairs in the rafters. (Courtesy SCV Historical Society.)

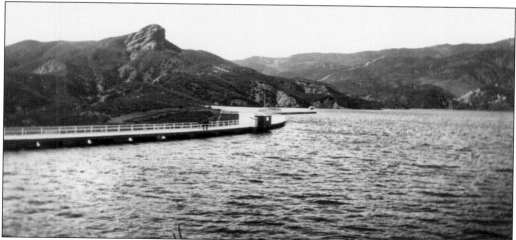

The St. Francis Dam, built to hold a year's supply of water for Los Angeles, held 18 billion gallons of water. Besides the carnage and loss of valuable farm topsoil along a 60-mile swath, there was the unspeakable toll of lives lost. Come dawn, fishermen near Oxnard, where the dam waters emptied, reported an epic shark feeding frenzy on animals and humans. (Courtesy SCV Historical Society.)

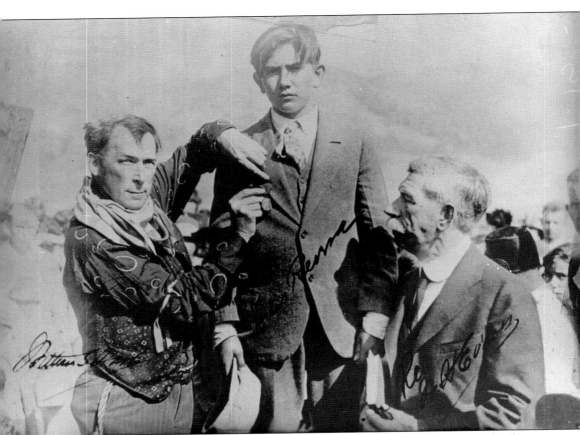

Silent superstar William S. Hart rode about town on horseback, aiding in the rescue. The thespian was moved to tears when he found the body of a five-year-old boy. He arranged for the child to be buried in a tiny cowboy outfit. Here Hart (left) gives a medal to Luis Rivera who saved lives that horrible night when the St. Francis broke. The man to the right is Rev. Wolcott Evans, who earned the nickname "Shepherd of the Hills." Since becoming minister of the Newhall Presbyterian Church in 1914, he was one of the most influential people of the SCV, quietly ministering to people of all faiths while living in poverty. In his old age, he would call on people in his rickety buckboard. The town, and Hart, got together and bought him a brand-new car. Small trivia: while hunting in the remote woods of North Dakota, Evans bumped into Theodore Roosevelt. Interestingly, the former president used to visit the SCV to hunt. (Courtesy SCV Historical Society.)

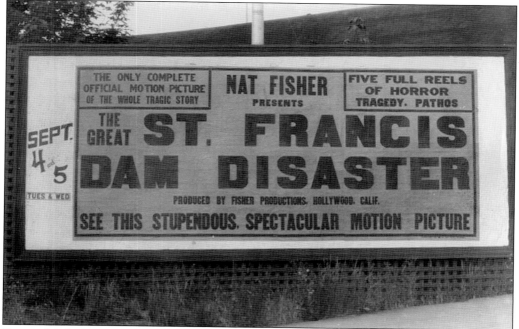

Except for the *Los Angeles Times* and the *Newhall Signal*, nearly every newspaper in America wrongly reported that the entire SCV was a "sunken Atlantis" and underwater. With the valley stunned, local businesses, like the Newhall Pharmacy, quickly hawked commemorative gifts and a movie was quickly made. (Courtesy SCV Historical Society.)

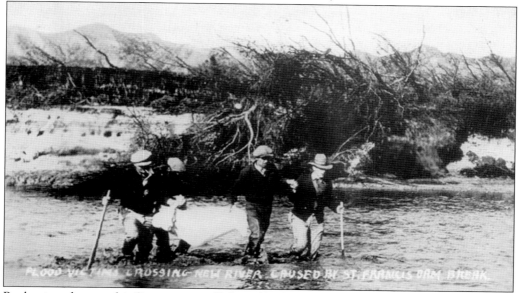

By the time the wave hit Castaic, it was 60 feet tall. The next morning, residents had to ford a new river. Fourteen years later, they were still finding victims. A prospector digging for gold in 1942 found the lower half of a human skeleton sticking up in the creek. There was no identification, but the bones were estimated to have been attached to something corporeal about 15 years earlier. (Courtesy SCV Historical Society.)

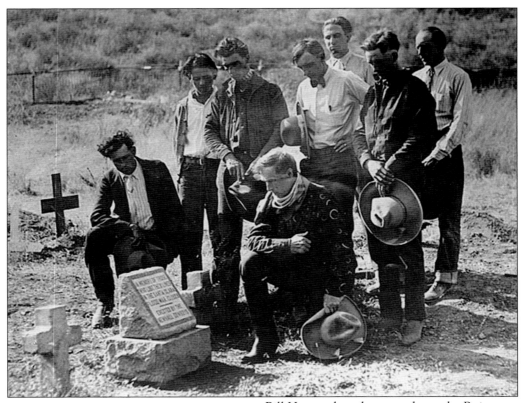

Bill Hart and cowboys ponder at the Ruiz Cemetery. Another famous actor, Harry Carey, lost much of his ranch but not his home to floodwaters. Carey told *Signal* editor Fred Trueblood that his Native American medicine man had a nightmare of impending disaster before the St. Francis Dam burst. About 100 Navajo workers on Carey's ranch respected the omen and left for Arizona three days before. (Courtesy SCV Historical Society.)

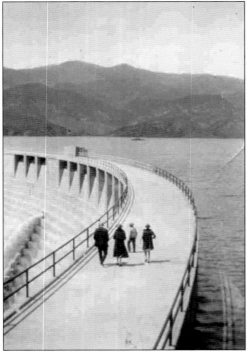

Time heals. Some small humor remains. The morning after, young Bailey Haskell (of Haskell Canyon fame) rescued a teenage girl. Nude from the floodwaters, she clutched to the branches of a mighty oak. "Bailes" propped up a ladder, climbed the tree, threw a blanket over her, and carried her fireman style. Haskell recalled before he died, "Seventy years later she's still embarrassed and won't talk to me." (Courtesy SCV Historical Society.)

Eight

BRONCO BUSTERS TO SODBUSTERS

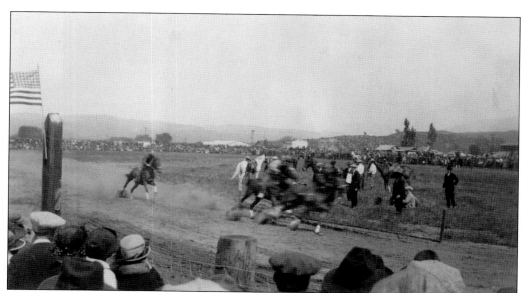

Since the early 1920s, the SCV was home to one of the world's largest rodeos. It started where Newhall Elementary sits today with impresario "Cowboy" Bob Anderson raking in $1,000 (mostly in coin) on an almost impromptu event. The rodeo moved to the current Saugus Speedway and, over the years, was known by many names. (Courtesy SCV Historical Society.)

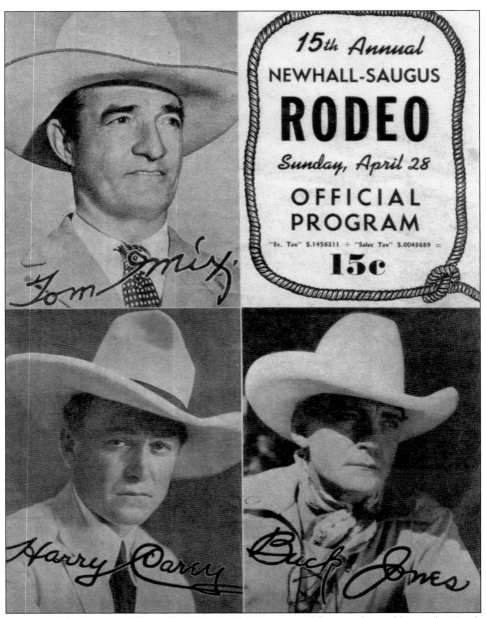

15th Annual
NEWHALL-SAUGUS
RODEO
Sunday, April 28
OFFICIAL
PROGRAM
"Ex. Tax" $.1456311 + "Sales Tax" $.0043689 =
15¢

As a vision of the future, traffic gridlock hit the SCV as tens of thousands would visit the Newhall-Saugus rodeo. Perhaps the most spectacular event was the 15th annual, held in 1940. John Wayne was on the board of directors. Tom Mix was president. Errol Flynn, Clark Gable, Lucille Ball, Gary Cooper, Jack Benny, and a host of Hollywood who's who attended. Mix raced Western star Buck Jones in a chariot race in downtown Newhall. Jones would later die (along with this author's uncle) in the Coconut Grove fire. SCV's common faces—Jones, Hart, Carey, and Mix—would all die within a few years of each other. Actor/cowboy Slim Pickens was a rodeo clown and wild-cow milker. Future Academy Award–winner Ben Johnson (*The Last Picture Show*) took second in bronc riding. One of Hollywood's biggest stars, Hoot Gibson, had owned the rodeo grounds, which today is the Saugus Speedway. (Courtesy SCV Historical Society.)

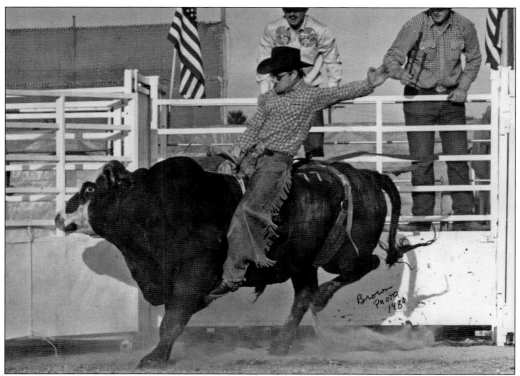

A *Signal* reporter noted, "The SPCA has taken most of the joy out of steer wrestling." The old form was invented by famed black cowboy Bill Pickett. He invented the style of vaulting from his horse, grabbing the steer by the horns, twisting them 180 degrees, then biting the steer on the lips to pull it down. Above, a bull rider at Frontier Days tries to stay on for eight seconds. (Courtesy SCV Historical Society.)

"Big" Bill Bonelli bought the rodeo grounds after the floods of 1938. He also headed the state Board of Equalization. He wrote *Billion Dollar Blackjack*, an indictment on the *Los Angeles Times* and their liquor and real estate holdings. Bonelli would live on his million-acre Mexican ranch for 17 years, hiding out on trumped-up tax charges. He was given a letter of apology by the IRS. (Courtesy Alan Pollack.)

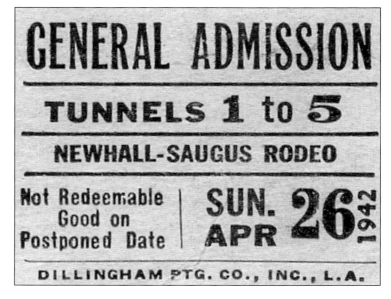

GENERAL ADMISSION

TUNNELS 1 to 5

NEWHALL-SAUGUS RODEO

Not Redeemable Good on Postponed Date

SUN. APR 26 1942

DILLINGHAM PTG. CO., INC., L.A.

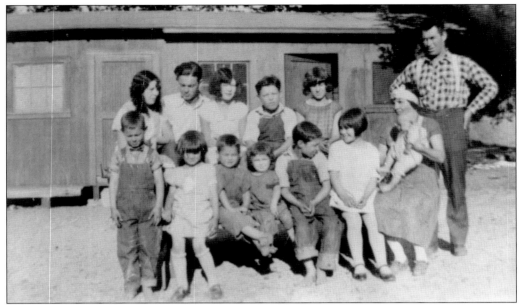

Homesteader Frank Walker and his huge family managed to live in a tiny two-room cabin in Placerita Canyon. In 1938, state and federal governments agreed to create Placerita Canyon National Park. Using water from the aqueduct, they would create a sprawling greenbelt with man-made lakes, campgrounds, and waterfalls. World War II came, and the project was forgotten. (Courtesy SCV Historical Society.)

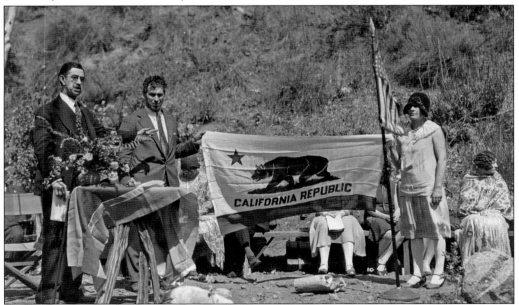

Frank and Hortense Walker hold the Bear Flag as Adolph Rivera speaks during the dedication of Placerita Canyon as a state historical monument and scenic wonder. In 1971, Los Angeles County Regional Planning Commission announced a plan to turn the road into a four-lane freeway and concrete Placerita Creek. It never happened. Golden Oak Ranch, Disney's movie location, is across the street. (Courtesy SCV Historical Society.)

Country children sometimes have the most unusual toys. One of Frank Walker's children plays lariat with a snake at her Placerita Canyon home in the 1930s. Her dad was an industrious soul, eking out a living from everything from pumping oil to harvesting shingle rock. (Courtesy SCV Historical Society.)

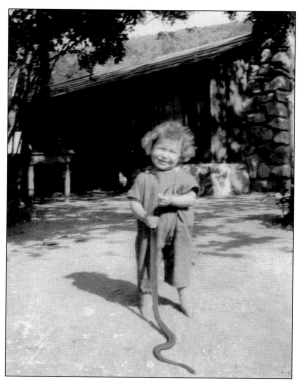

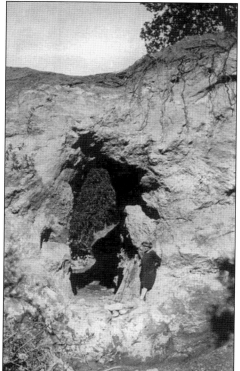

Placerita Canyon is still a natural wonderland with hiking trails next to a seasonal creek and paths ascending into bear and mountain lion territory. Up until the 1960s, the canyon used to have a rare natural land bridge. Teen vandals took shovels and destroyed it. (Courtesy SCV Historical Society.)

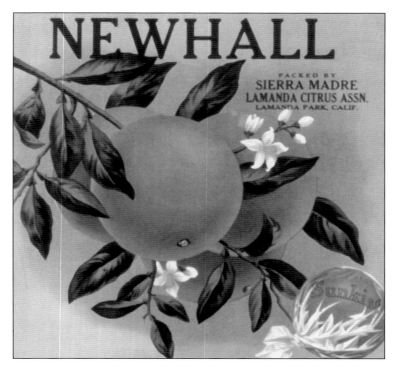

In the 1950s, Paul Hackney, orchard manager of Walter D. Newhall's spread, developed a new orange called the Newhall Strain. Hackney noted an unusual hybrid branch, made cuttings, and grew it at his home on the Newhall Ranch and grafted them. Hackney noted that the new orange was better colored and larger and had a higher sugar content. The varmints liked the new orange, too. In 1953, rats chewed up and destroyed 150 of the trees. (Courtesy Newhall Land.)

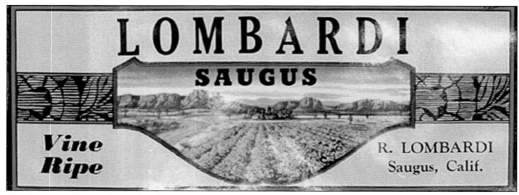

The Lombardi Ranch used to be a good-sized family operation, but with progress comes specialization. Every autumn, thousands now flock to the Bouquet Canyon farm to buy one kind of vegetable: the Halloween pumpkin. The Lombardis have turned their spread into a small amusement park, with tractor rides for big and small. (Courtesy Leon Worden.)

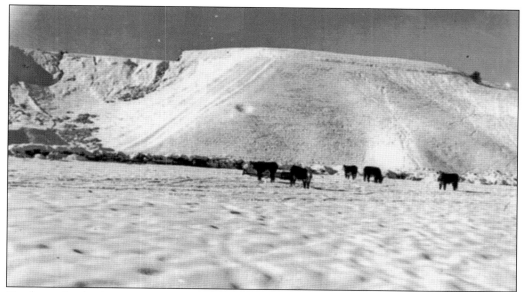

Cattle grazing in the snow are a rare picture for modern Santa Clarita. There's rarely snow. There's rarely cattle. In the mid-20th century, there were 10 working big commercial dairies here, but there are zero today. In 1917, cattle also brought people closer together. The entire valley—cows and people—was quarantined by the National Guard for a hoof-and-mouth outbreak. Folks spent months visiting each other and eating chicken. (Courtesy SCV Historical Society.)

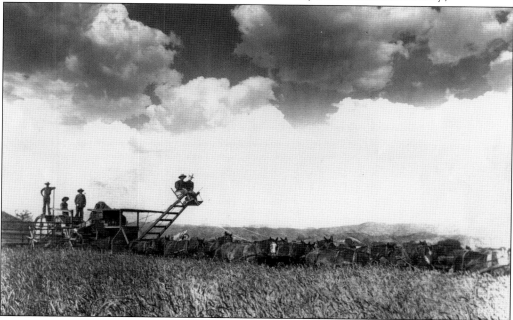

Gone are the days of big-time agriculture in the SCV. Usually gypsies and migrant workers from Mexico harvested crops. In 1943, there was a mix-up. No one was available to harvest tons of potatoes. Businesses and schools closed early, and everyone in town pitched in. A few years back, Newhall Land and Farming Company dropped the last 17 characters to their handle, shortening their name to Newhall Land. They stopped farming. (Courtesy SCV Historical Society.)

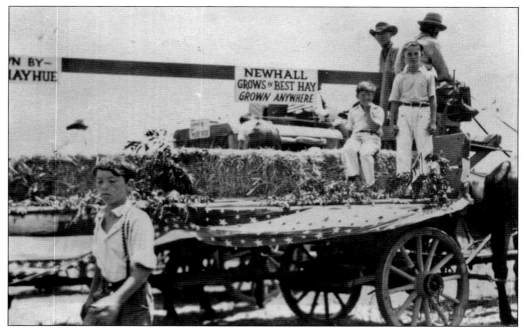

Agriculture was a big theme in the SCV's Fourth of July parade. Born a pauper, William Mayhue (not pictured) made and lost several fortunes before dying penniless in a government home for the aged. His wife, Pallie, was a cook in Mentryville. One day she watched, in horror, as an oil worker took off his boots to knead bread dough in a washtub—with his feet. (Courtesy SCV Historical Society.)

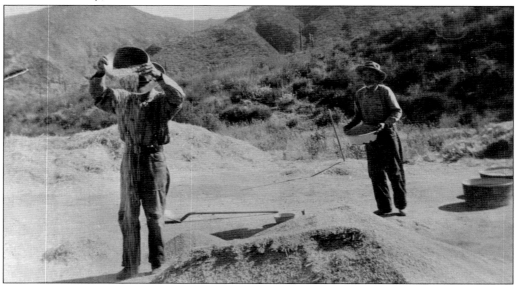

This is sifting wheat the hard way. In 1970, there were about 3,000 acres locally used for agriculture. That worked out to about $6 million in food produced, from watermelon to alfalfa, plus the valley sustained 17,500 acres available for grazing and planting, which included Christmas tree farms ($150,000 in sales in 1975). In 1958, more than 8,000 acres were harvested and income was $3.9 million. (Courtesy SCV Historical Society.)

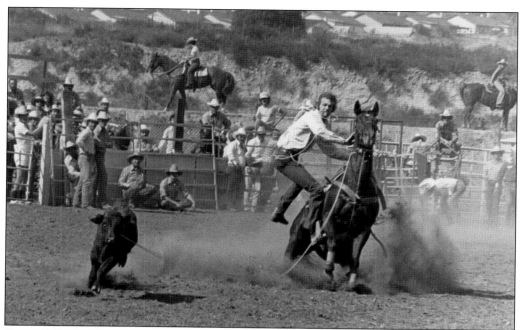

Since 1962, the Canyon Country Chamber of Commerce sponsored Frontier Days, a big salute to things Western. It boasted of burro races, parades, and carnivals and grew to a huge event attracting many. The last rodeo staged in the SCV was back in the 1980s. Earlier, Wild West re-enactors accidentally used live ammo and shot five audience members. On the bright side, they were from out of town. (Courtesy SCV Historical Society.)

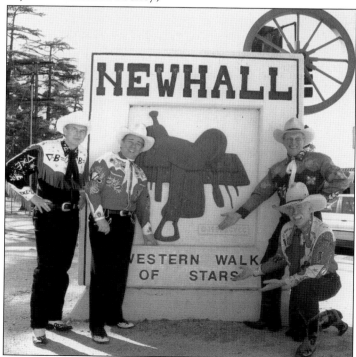

While there are hardly any working ranches or farms in the valley today, the city of Santa Clarita keeps its Western heritage alive with one of the planet's largest events of its kind: the Cowboy Fest. The city also now hosts the Western Walk of Stars, a salute to those contributing to the SCV's cowboy roots, like the famed Western band Riders in the Sky. (Courtesy City of Santa Clarita.)

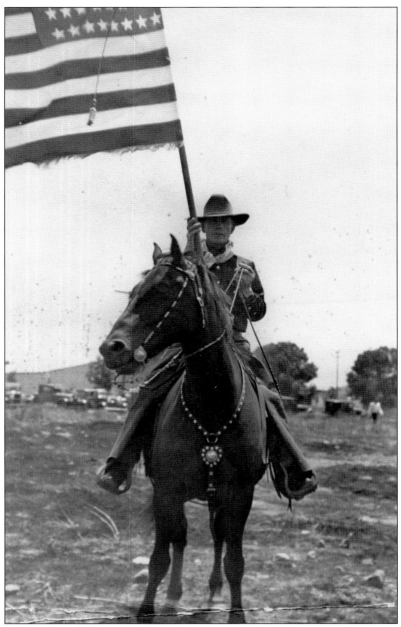

History often remembers the infamous but rarely the simple good man. Charles Kingsbury was a prizefighter who lied about his age to fight in the Spanish-American War and started the local Kiwanis. Coming here in 1919, he worked on the big state water projects and had his own butcher's shop. But mainly, Kingsbury was famous around the valley for his big heart. He was noted for his lifetime work that no local child would see Christmas without a present. Kingsbury had a go-around with the Federal government. He was informed that they had no record of him existing and that he needed to provide a birth certificate as an alibi for his whereabouts in 1892. A couple of other old-timers kidded Kingsbury, asking whether he had been born or he had been hatched. He died in 1963. His home is a shrine at Heritage Junction. (Courtesy SCV Historical Society.)

Nine

NEWHALLYWOOD

SCVians Harry Carey and William S. Hart died
within months of one another in 1946. Hart left
his entire estate to Los Angeles County, thereby
cutting out his son, Bill Hart Jr. Few remember
that Bill Sr.'s death created a decade-long series of
sensational trials for control of the ranch and the
multi-million-dollar estate. The case often reached
comic proportions. It took two days to read one
hypothetical question into the record. It was
15,000 words in length, covering 72 pages. Hart
Jr. had stopped his father's cremation, which was
in process, running in with a court order for his
dad's brain. The case shed uncomfortable light and
juicy details on Hart Sr.'s winter-spring relationship
with teen actress and his only wife Winifred
Westover. After losing the primo property in the
SCV, Hart Jr. became a real estate appraiser. There
were two-dozen attorneys speaking during the
case. Rumor was that Hart Jr. and Westover were
backed by local wealthy oilman Y. A. Yant, who
wanted to drill for petroleum under the future
county park. (Courtesy SCV Historical Society.)

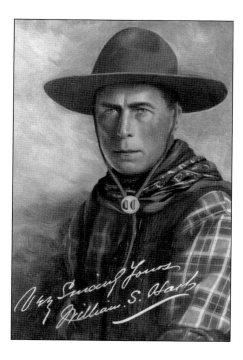

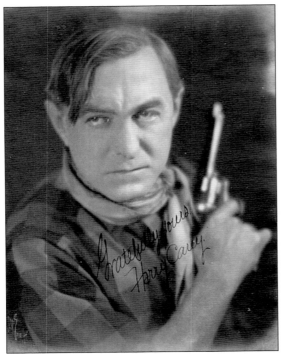

Harry Carey was one of the rare actors who successfully transferred from superstar silent status to the talkies. He made nearly 300 movies and owned a ranch sprawling over 3,000 acres in scenic San Francisquito Canyon. His friend and visitor Will Rogers called him "The greatest cowboy ever in pictures." Today his ranch house is a county park in Tesoro del Valle. (Courtesy Jack Stewart/Harry Carey Jr.)

While filming a Western in territorial Arizona in the 1910s, Carey made friends with the *Diné*—meaning "the people"—also known as the Navajo. Carey brought back the entire village of 80 to work as cowboys, cooks, artisans, and shepherds at his ranch and resort. Carey's place was then on the main road to Central California and housed a dude ranch, restaurant, and general store. (Courtesy Jack Stewart/Harry Carey Jr.)

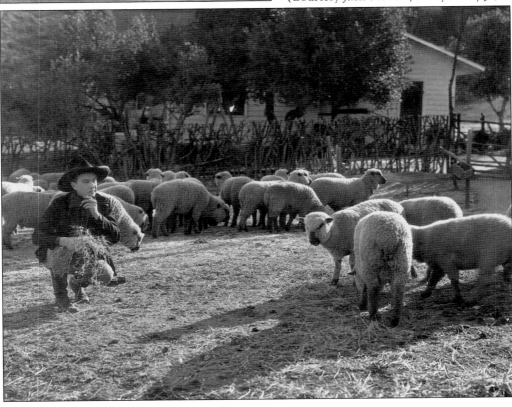

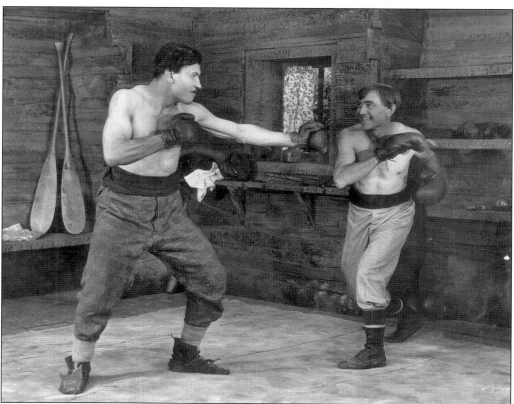

Carey was one of the most popular figures in Hollywood, friend to major stars, wrestlers, and every decent cowboy in the SCV. While his original house dodged the St. Francis Dam flood, a few years later, it burned to the ground, along with a one-copy-only novel Carey had finished. He graduated from NYU and was starting tackle on their 1898 and 1899 football teams. (Courtesy Jack Stewart/Harry Carey Jr.)

The Navajo had their own village on Carey's ranch and hosted an annual rodeo. In the 1920s, they also fielded their own semipro baseball team, playing the likes of Tom Mix's squad and the Apemen, who were owned by Tarzan creator Edgar Rice Burroughs, on their Saugus baseball diamond. Carey's son was noted actor Harry Carey Jr., who grew up on the ranch. (Courtesy Jack Stewart/Harry Carey Jr.)

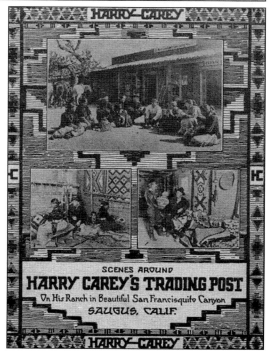

SCENES AROUND
HARRY CAREY'S TRADING POST
On His Ranch in Beautiful San Francisquito Canyon
SAUGUS, CALIF.

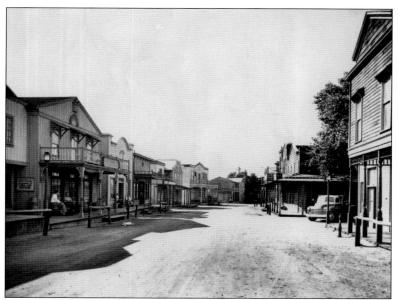

Melody Ranch is one of the world's oldest movie studios. It was originally located about a mile up Placerita Canyon from where it sits today. The HBO series *Deadwood* was filmed here, the latest in a series of hundreds of Westerns. James Arness marched down this dusty Main Street every week to start the television series *Gunsmoke*. Before starting a multi-million-dollar beauty business, Max Factor was a makeup artist. His tent is still there. Joel McCrea (William S. Hart's paperboy), Bruce Willis, John Wayne, Gary Cooper (in *High Noon*), Errol Flynn, and even Hollywood's worst director, Ed Wood, made movie magic on this lot. The Mexican Chapel (below) was lost to fire and rebuilt a few years ago. It was featured in the film and series *Zorro*. Remember those countless old Republic and Monogram films? Many were shot here. (Above courtesy Melody Ranch Studio; below courtesy A. B. Perkins.)

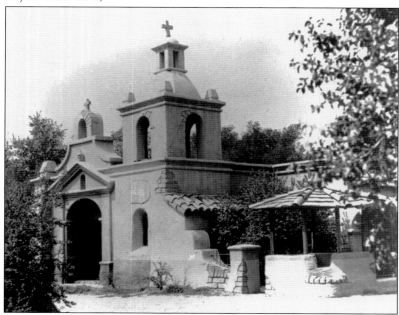

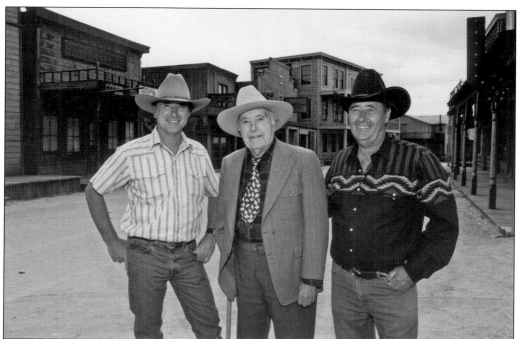

Will Rogers stumbled upon a train clerk named Orvon singing in an Oklahoma train depot. Rogers chastised him that with a voice like that he should be in pictures. By 1934, Orvon Autry was at Melody Ranch, filming a sci-fi Western series. The producers made him use his middle name, Gene. The "Singing Cowboy" returned in 1952 to buy the movie lot and was going to use the location for his Western Heritage Museum, now in Glendale. After his death, Gene Autry's second wife, Jackie, sold off pieces of the original 110-acre studio until only 22 acres remained. Above, the Veluzat family, from left to right, Andre, Paul, and Renaud, bought and restored it. Andre and Renaud are brothers. Paul passed away recently at 101. He was a former bodyguard to J. Paul Getty and the oldest living Texas Ranger. (Above courtesy Melody Ranch Studio; below courtesy Leon Worden.)

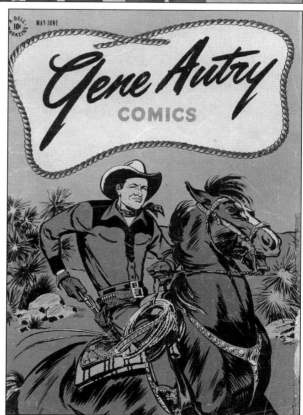

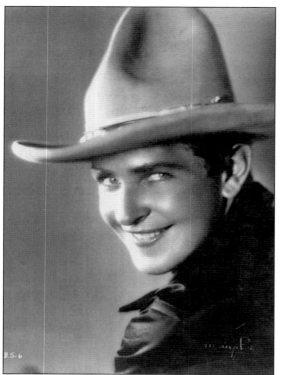

Youthful box office hero Robert Bradbury Jr. (Bob Steele, left) would bring a tagalong friend, Marion Morrison, to the Placeritos studio. With a name-change to John Wayne, the "Duke" would become the screen's first singing cowboy (as "Singing Sandy" Saunders in *Riders of Destiny*, 1933). Melody did not just make Westerns. Bela Lugosi, Boris Karloff, and even Jennifer Lopez filmed here. In 1962, a 10,000-acre blaze obliterated most of Melody Ranch. The house where W. C. Field's filmed *My Little Chickadee* was saved by a bucket brigade manned by Elvis Presley. Later the Veluzat family would use Wayne—literally—to reconstruct the lot. With dozens of photographs of the Duke standing in various entryways and buildings, Wayne was the boilerplate for reconstruction. Interestingly, right after the fire, a television crew used the charred wreckage to create a European bombed-out city. (Above courtesy Melody Ranch; below courtesy Fred Trueblood II of the *Signal*.)

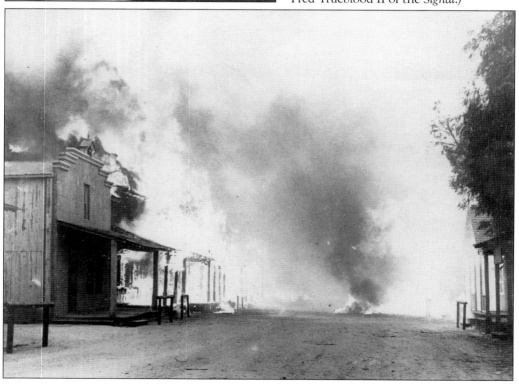

Famed comedian W. C. Fields used to live on Eighth Street in one of the Charlie Mack stone houses, across from Bill Hart. Mack was famous as part of the vaudeville/radio blackface duo the Black Crows. Mack had started building an artist haven, and the unique homes are still there. One recently sported a front-gate sign warning inquiring land agents, "Realtors Will Be Shot." (Courtesy SCV Historical Society.)

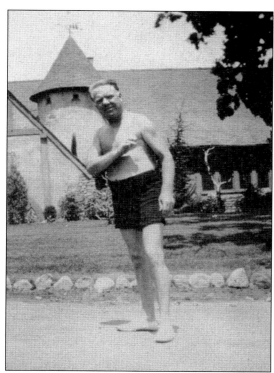

Frank Edwin Churchill's Paradise Ranch was right next door to the huge Castaic Brick factory. Besides creating "Who's Afraid of the Big Bad Wolf," the single most successful cartoon song ever, Oscar-winning Churchill wrote many songs for Walt Disney. He committed suicide in 1942. The new Paradise Ranch owners threw away all his original sheet music, worth a small fortune today. (Courtesy SCV Historical Society.)

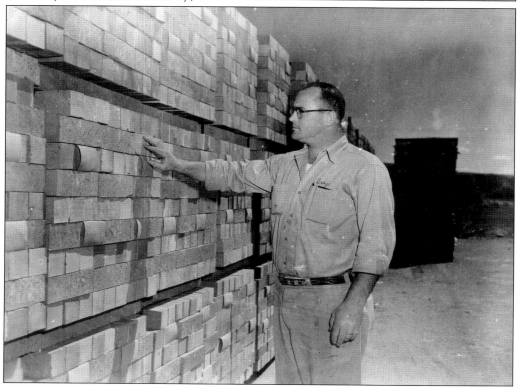

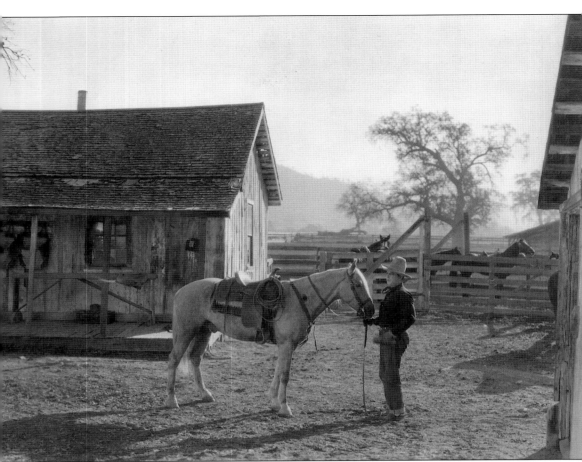

Edmund Richard "Hoot" Gibson was a true world-famous rodeo star who owned the Saugus Rodeo Grounds on Soledad Canyon Road. He had been making films in the SCV with friends Tom Mix and Ken Maynard here since 1915. Hoot and Ken once hurt themselves in an air race crash. In 1943, Hoot and Maynard noted that they were tired of the recent slate of cowboy actors "with lavender pants" and filmed eight Westerns locally. Hoot was quoted, "And all of a sudden, somebody seemed to have decided that maybe cowboys ought to ride horses." Hoot would show up at Newhall Elementary to watch his movies with kids. Next to Mix, Gibson was the second top-box-office star in the world. The all-around world-champion cowboy made, and lost, a fortune and ended up being a greeter in Las Vegas. (Courtesy Jack Stewart/Dobey Carey.)

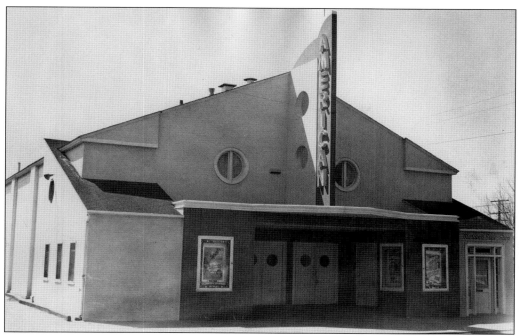

Silent star William S. Hart donated the land and several thousand dollars and acquired the services of master theater architect S. Charles Lee to build the American Theater. The grand opening was delayed in 1941 because hobos had broken in and used molding to start a fire inside. It closed as a theater in 1965. The American Legion still operates it as a clubhouse and banquet hall. (Courtesy SCV Historical Society.)

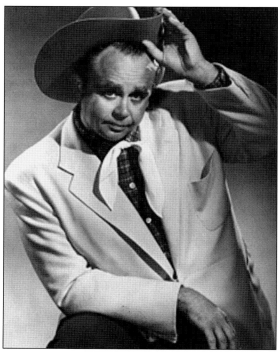

One of Sand Canyon's most famous figures was music producer Cliffie Stone. His 1950s *Hometown Jamboree* was the number one show on television. Stone was famous for hosting huge free concerts, bringing some of the biggest country/western talents in the country. Enshrined in the Nashville Country Music Hall of Fame, he managed Tennessee Ernie Ford, Molly Bee, Tex Williams, and dozens of other performers. (Courtesy SCV Historical Society.)

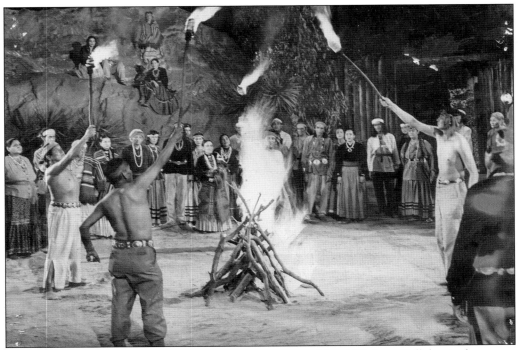

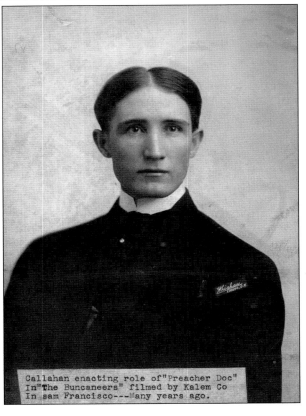

It's said Robert Callahan's ghost still haunts the 12-acre site of his old Wild West Frontier Village. The tourist attraction and community center housed the Dead Shot Saloon, Klondike Kate's Crib, Hangtown Hall, and a museum. Located way up the Sierra Highway, it was the home of the Canyon Theatre Guild for years. Callahan wrote the original *Lone Ranger* and *Death Valley Days* on radio and is credited with creating California's first theme park—Callahan's Old West—in Culver City in the 1920s. Above, an enthusiastic production of *Ramona* is staged at the Sierra Highway compound. Interestingly, the "birthplace" of Ramona is across the valley, at Camulos Ranch. (Both courtesy SCV Historical Society.)

Callahan enacting role of "Preacher Doc" In "The Buccaneers" filmed by Kalem Co In sam Francisco---Many years ago.

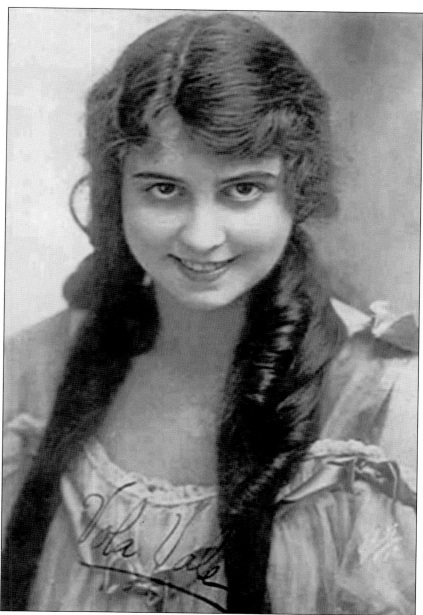

There is no reason why anyone should remember Vola Vale. She made about 60 silent movies, some opposite William S. Hart. She is important in reporting the Santa Clarita heritage in that she represents the forgotten. While Hollywood makes more mediocre films than good ones, there are factors both magical and economic. Since the start of the 20th century, movie companies have been visiting the SCV. Jackie Chan's production company recently moved here. Movies bring money to Newhall Paint for set designs or give work to makeup artists like Eugenia Weston or Mary Phillips. Cowboy Andy Jauregui was paid to teach Clark Gable to throw a lariat. Cameron Denzel and Corky Randall trained horses for the celluloid. From sandwiches to pickup trucks to tax dollars, movies have been sometimes an eyesore to behold, sometimes an invisible bull's-eye only a genius can see, but always a boon to the community. (Courtesy Leon Worden.)

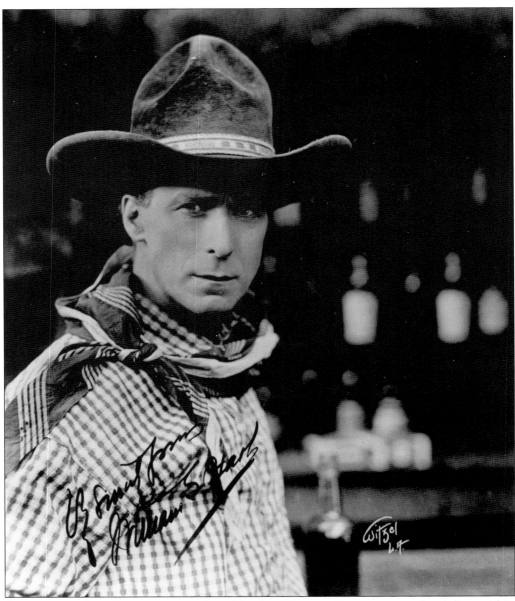

Stars come and go. Some are remembered fondly. Others strike a resonant chord deep within people. What made William S. Hart have such a lasting and profound effect on the American psyche was a combination of things. He used a lifetime of studying classic drama and, in that, brought to life classic truths. Hart played the great heroes and villains of Shakespeare, then molded them into an authentic frontier hero. What makes a hero? Misunderstood and doomed to failure, a hero tries anyway. A hero puts another's needs ahead of his or her own. They protect the land and those weaker than them. It's a classic knight's code of right and wrong that exemplifies the best part of America in the past. A hero is the answer to Hamlet's question: "To be, or not to be." A hero does. Over the years, many actors tackling Western roles thank William S. Hart for creating the boilerplate of the American cowboy hero. That better image Hart helped to spread is still seen around the world today. (Courtesy SCV Historical Society.)

Ten

THEY SING THE BODY ECLECTIC

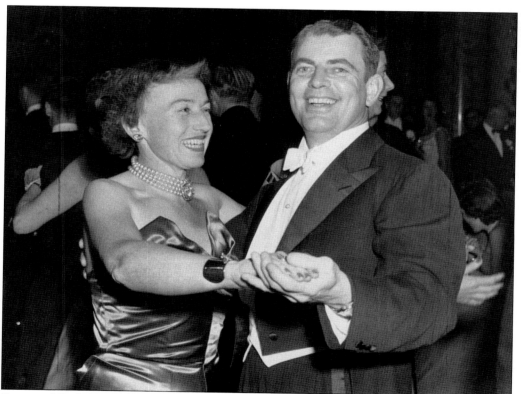

Scott and Ruth Newhall were the closest to royalty this valley has ever seen. They were world explorers, amateur archeologists, and just wicked enough that the public was powerless to turn away. They were not so much editors as madcap emperors of some forgotten and wealthy duchy. With their son, Tony, they held a creative 25-year reign over the valley through their newspaper, the *Newhall Signal.* (Courtesy Tony Newhall.)

The Newhall Signal

$2.00 For the Year   DEVOTED TO THE NEWHALL-SAUGUS VALLEYS   Build Up, Don't Tear |

Vol. I.   Newhall, California, Friday, February 7, 1919

PERSHING UP ON FRENCH CUSTOMS

American General Claims Admiration of the People.

KISSES OLD FRENCH LADY

Round Smack on the Two Cheeks of Dear Old Lady Who Made Speech Expressing Gratitude of People to Americans—Acquires Such Facility in the Language That He Can Now Make Good Speech in French.

General Pershing has kissed "une Francaise"—French scholars notice the gender. This was no official embrace of a bearded general. It was a round smack on the two cheeks of a dear old French lady.

General Pershing is known to have acquired such remarkable facility in the French language that he makes a rattling good speech in French to-day. It remained for "Le Carnet de la Semaine," a French weekly paper, to reveal that the general in chief of the Yank forces has not lagged behind his subordinates in acquiring French expressions. In a recent issue Le Carnet says:

"General Pershing is a great American. Learned, restrained, always calm, he symbolizes that American simplicity which looks on and learns. "The general's manners likewise are characterized by the most spontaneous frankness and his actions remain graven in the memory of those who have seen him.

Kisses Old French Lady.

"At D——, General Pershing arrived recently with his staff. The armistice had been signed the evening before — delirious enthusiasm, ovations. In this little northern village a little crowd quickly surrounded the glorious American liberators and their chief. Such a riot ensued that an old mistress of ceremonies raised herself amid the rout and demanded silence so that, in the name of all, she might thank the general. Silence was restored and an old woman, a very old and trembling little woman, approached him in all her dignity and murmured words of gratitude. As she went on she became confused with the unaccustomed honor. Her words became mixed. Finally, knowing nothing else to do, she suddenly seized both hands of General Pershing and shook them heartily.

"And the general mutually squeezed the two hands of the old lady. Then suddenly, without a word, he removed

FAIRBANK'S NEW FILM

Douglas Fairbanks and his company of about two hundred, came up from Los Angeles Tuesday by special train and autos and pulled off a moving picture stunt. We did not learn the name of the future film, but judging from what we saw, "Douglas at the County Fair" might be considered appropriate. The location chosen for the taking of the pictures was the vacant ground lying west of the depot. Market street from the drug store to the railroad track, was decorated with yards and yards of bunting, signs, flags, etc., not omitting the "ice cream" stands along the way. There were about forty horses in the performance and these did their part by going through the antics which people pay to see at a county fair. A "special train" met by the committee was an interesting feature.

Altogether the performance at "Fairpoint," which was the name Newhall assumed for the day, was very entertaining and we did not have to pay the price of a ticket either.

OUR HEALTH OFFICER MAKES A VISIT

The Stearling Borax Mine, near Lang, are working full time, three sets of miners working eight hours each, consequently the mine never stops working. Forty-five men are now employed and the town has an air of industry. The men are all loyal and devoted to their Superintendent, Mr. Stewart. They all look prosperous and contented. The Colony was visited last week by our local Health Officer, Dr. Geo. Stevenson, who inspected the school children, reports no sickness, and the healthiest bunch of youngsters he ever met.

Mrs. Stewart, wife of the Superintendent, acts as godmother over the children, looking after their physical needs while Miss Lemon, the amiable and competent school teacher, is very proud of the progress the children are making in their studies. Our Health Officer, Dr. Stevenson, and Mr. Chas. Houghton, the druggist, were welcomed and entertained by the officers of the Company to which they return thanks for the same.

Berlin.'

"'In Berlin! Then you will go there, madame!' cried the general to Madame Poincare.

"Then they talked of other things

THE LOCAL NEWS ITEMS

"Say, can't you send us in some school notes each week?"

There have been several cases of the "flu" here, but they are all up and around now.

Mr. Buttler of the Buttler Grocery was in Los Angeles the first of the week buying goods.

Mr. L. G. Pullen, our genial barber, was in Los Angeles Monday buying stock for his cigar stand.

We have had scarcely if any rain so far this season and the farmers are praying for more moisture.

The five-year-old son of Mr. and Mrs. Thomas M. Frena, who has been very sick with pneumonia, is rapidly improving.

Mr. Bricker, of the Bricker Grocery, was in San Fernando on Monday. He is kept quite busy with his truck business.

E. S. Chrisfield is repairing the house which he recently purchased on Walnut street. When these changes are completed, the place will be occupied by ye editor and family.

Dr. G. F. Stevenson, health officer for this section, made our office a pleasant call the first of the week, and in the matter of count stands No. 1 on our list of subscribers.

Mr. Bucknell, manager of the Newhall Lumber Co., and family, spent Sunday in Los Angeles with friends and relatives.

We are strangers here, and if those knowing of items of interest will kindly bring them to this office, it will greatly assist us in maknig our columns more interesting.

Mr. W. W. Hooper, of Brawley, Cal., an old mining engineer, is stopping at Hotel Swall. Mr. Hooper is not feeling very well and is here for his health. He has many words of praise for our climate.

We understand that there will be services in the Presbyterian church next Sunday, the first time for eight weeks, which was also closed on account of the "Flu." It is understood Pastor Evans will speak.

SHIPS FIRST IN FRANCE'S NEE

Must Have Aid in Restoring chant Marine.

VAST LOSSES SUMME

Edward de Billy, Deputy High missioner of the French Repu the United States, Gives Sta of Country's Needs—2,500, Her Young Men Killed or M 26,000 Factories Ruined.

With 2,500,000 of her yo ablest, and most spirited men k maimed, and upward of half her try and shipping destroyed war, France's appeal to the alli ing the period of rehabilitation for help in rebuilding the facto farms which the Germans wreck for assistance in constructing chasing ships, said Edward de deputy high commissioner of French republic.

Admitting his country's gain conflict, in the revitalizing French spirit of self-confidenc dued by the defeat of 1871, and embracing Alsace and Lorraine, wi agricultural districts, Mr. de Bi the war's losses were far great denied that France was "bled but said the handicap impose result of her sacrifices in resist invader could not be overcome with outside aid.

Resorting to figures, he d that 26,000 factories in the Fre tricts occupied by the German destroyed or stripped of th chinery; that almost 12,000,00 of cattle were seized; that th of miles of farm land, devasta shells, was made unfit for culti that the net loss in ship t through sinkings and enforced ment in production, was 670,00 and that the money cost of t flict, in appropriations and pu aggregated 158,000,000,000 fra $31,000,000,000.

"Our army had to stand," h "the first rush of the invasion the other armies were being pr And, however wonderful was fort of the British, some month and afterward that of the A army, the front held by the had never been less than two-th the total line from the North the Swiss border. Thus our loss greater than those of any othe A part of our country has b vaded, its population treated as their houses looted, their facto

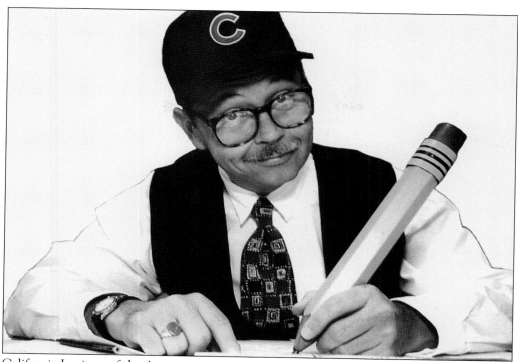

California Institute of the Arts graduate Randy Ray Wicks died at an early age but not before creating an unusual legacy. He was noted by his cartooning colleagues and the nation's major media as one of the world's top political cartoonists. One thing that set Wicks apart was his output: six to seven cartoons a week, and each one was a home run. Also, the award-winning Wicks turned down many offers from larger newspapers to work at the small Southern California daily the *Newhall Signal*. With a few deft strokes, Wicks could make readers cry or laugh, sometimes with the same illustration. Here he looks at the nation's military heritage on Memorial Day and the passing of Muppets creator Jim Henson. His life's collection is at the Valencia Library. A sampling of his work is in the book *The Worst of Wicks*. (Both courtesy the *Signal*.)

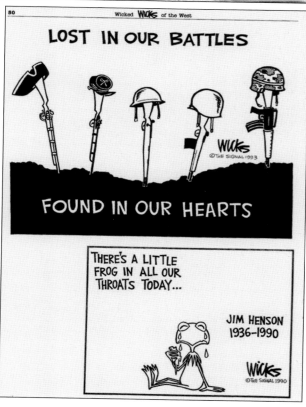

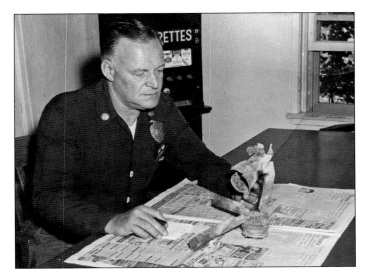

The local fire captain examines rocket shrapnel in the 1950s. The air force inadvertently attacked the SCV in August 1956 when it sent two F-89 jets to shoot down an out-of-control navy drone plane. The pilots fired 208 Tiny Tim rockets and missed every time. Several buildings and vehicles were hit and fires started, but no one was hurt. The drone crashed by itself in Palmdale. (Courtesy Time Ranger Collection.)

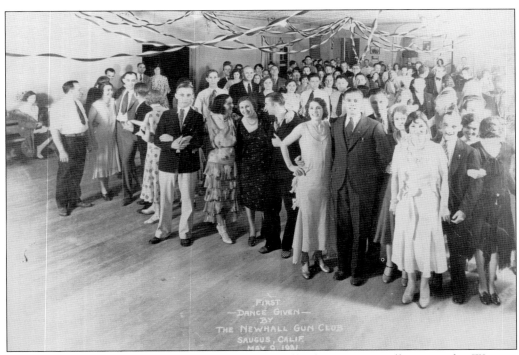

It wasn't baseball. It wasn't football. It wasn't basketball. The SCV was still very much a Western community up until the 1970s. One of the most popular events was the dance at the Newhall Gun Club. The Depression did not change the mood of these 1932 dancers. (Courtesy Time Ranger Collection.)

With its countless canyons, the Santa Clarita Valley attracted a bounty of moonshiners. During the brief reign of Prohibition, local farmers or organized crime figures dotted the landscape with illegal stills. A federal task force called the Dry Squad was centered here to bust up the bootleggers. The leader of the Dry Squad was James Bond (no, not that James Bond). (Courtesy Rushelle Summers.)

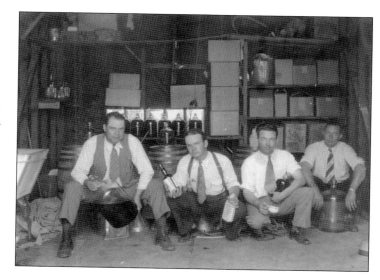

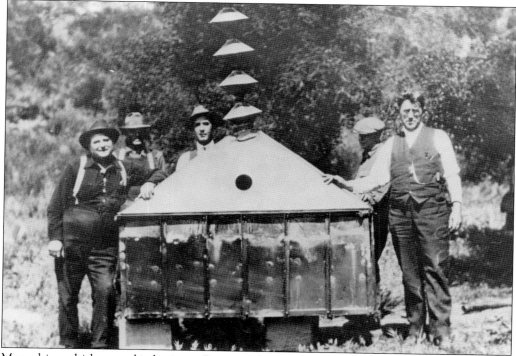

Moonshine whiskey was big business. Busts involving multiple giant 500- and 1,000-gallon stills were not uncommon. One local farmer was stunned with a $600 fine—the cost of a new house in 1923. Another rancher wept as 11,000 gallons of wine were dumped into a *barranca*. Two farmers/moonshiners socked Constable Jack Sanderson, giving him matching black eyes. He pistol-whipped the pair, sending them to Newhall Hospital. (Courtesy Rushelle Summers.)

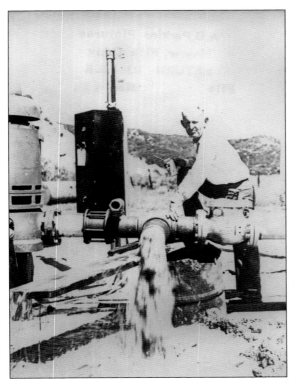

If it was not for A. B. Perkins, much of Santa Clarita's heritage would be lost. As a young man in the 1920s, he began tirelessly researching and cataloging information and photographs. He also ran the Newhall Water Company and was a renowned practical joker. Once a friend was getting a root canal. While he was unconscious, the scholar removed his shoes and socks and painted his feet red. (Courtesy A. B. Perkins.)

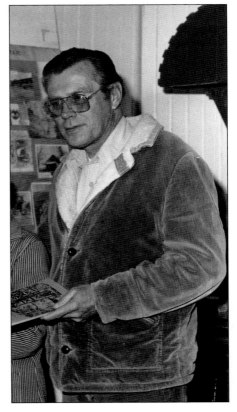

Gerald G. Reynolds picked up the mantle of historian A. B. Perkins, who died in 1977. "Jerry" had good qualifications for being a historian of the SCV. He had a delicious sense of humor, used to be a private eye, and he was an art historian who could draw. He organized the SCV Historical Society and began collecting the stories of the valley. Jerry died in 1996. (Courtesy SCV Historical Society.)

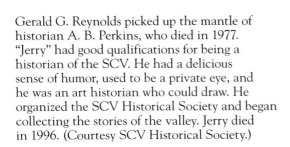

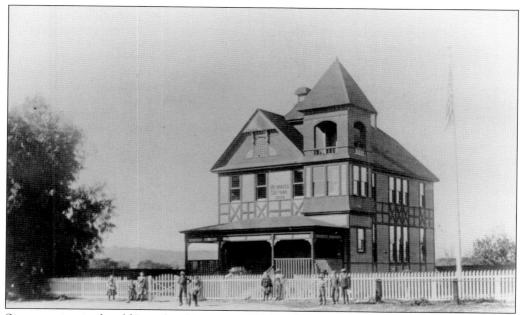

Since starting in the old Lyon bunkhouse in 1876, Newhall Elementary has turned out thousands of students. One was Buzz Barton (also known as Red Lameroux), the biggest child film star in America in the 1920s. In the 1910s, a Sunday church group that was renting the upstairs ran downstairs and attempted to lynch a man who had killed another in a fistfight. (Courtesy SCV Historical Society.)

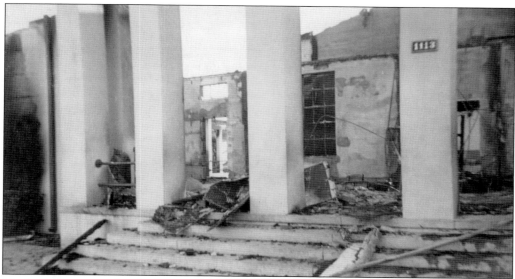

Newhall Elementary has both moved and burned to the ground several times, the last in 1939. Student Gus Trueblood recalled being lightly spanked by his father, *Newhall Signal* editor Fred Trueblood, not for being in a photograph dancing in front of the wreckage, but for that picture being on the cover of the *Los Angeles Times*. (Courtesy SCV Historical Society.)

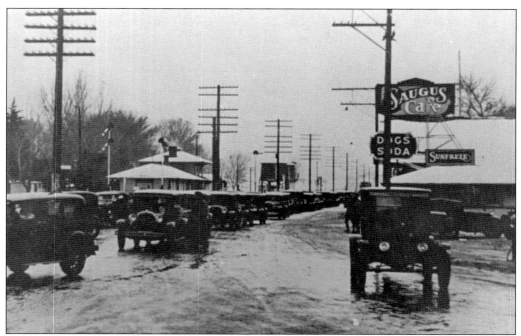

The Saugus Café is Los Angeles County's oldest continually operating eatery. Except for a remodeling and closure during World War II (due to food shortages), it has been open 24 hours for more than a century. Founded in 1887 inside the Saugus Train Station, it moved across the street in 1905 to its present location. When the St. Francis Dam burst in 1928, the owners were without power. They used hot water from a locomotive to make coffee for exhausted rescue workers. Hundreds of Hollywood muckety-mucks (John Wayne, John Ford, Gary Cooper) ate there. Judge Clarence MacDougal owned the café in the 1950s. Judge "Mac" was kidded because he became a judge before passing the bar exam. In fact, he had to take the test eight times. Below, a truck crashed into the adjunct Sandwich Shop on opening day in 1941. (Both courtesy A. B. Perkins.)

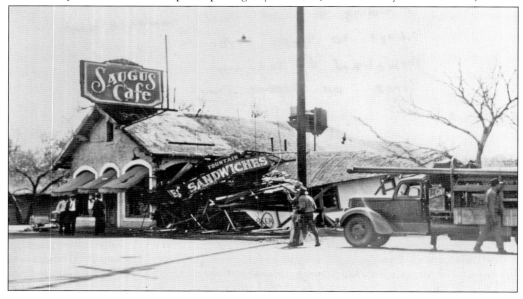

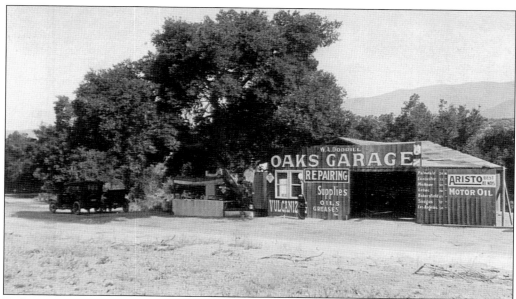

Today Le Chene is a famous Southland five-star French restaurant way up Sierra Highway in old Forrest Park. Seen above in 1916, the place was originally a gas station called Castle Rocks Service. Owner Bill Dodrill hauled the signature rocks from Little Rock in the 1920s by horse and wagon. It was a two-day trek—one way. The Oaks Café (below) of 1923 looks just like Le Chene today. In the 1940s, the place closed down. One time, a beekeeper's truck stalled; thousands of angry bees swarmed, in search of water, and stung most everything within several miles. Just down the road is another SCV famous eatery: the Halfway House. It's been seen in countless movies and television shows and got its name in the 1940s for being halfway between downtown Los Angeles and Lancaster. (Both courtesy SCV Historical Society.)

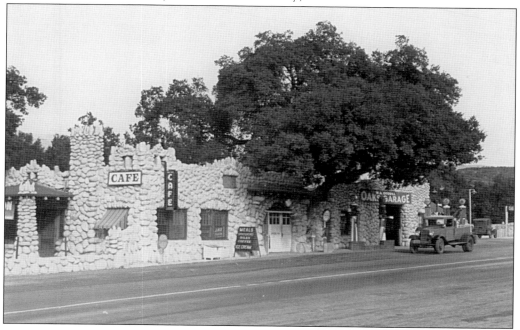

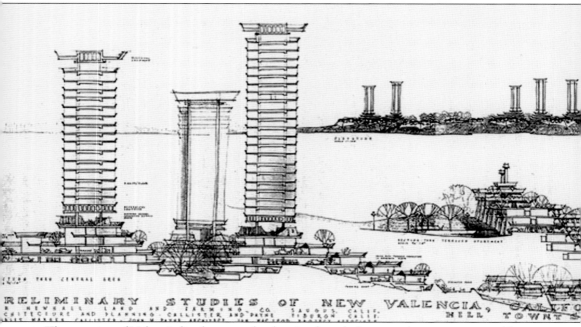

RELIMINARY STUDIES OF NEW VALENCIA, CALIFO NELL TOWNS

The concept of Valencia has been on the drawing boards for more than a century and has gone through many changes. In 1963, Newhall Land hired a San Francisco architectural critic to create "New Town." This original plan called for tenement-like skyscrapers housing about 200,000 people, surrounded by open space. Originally, Valencia was supposed to be connected—by a series of canals where neighbors could row to the grocery store. When they had the ribbon-cutting for a brand-new planned urban community in October 1965, the mayor of Valencia, Spain, was guest of honor. For the record, that would be Dr. Don Adolfo Rincon de Areliano. The eminent European heart surgeon (he worked from early morning to 11:30 a.m. as mayor then spent the rest of his day with family or at his practice) brought with him a tasseled bag of earth from his native city. Also on hand was the valley's honorary mayor, Judge C. M. MacDougall, who, obviously, did not have as far to drive. (Courtesy Newhall Land.)

Snow is rare indeed, coming about every 10 years to the SCV and not staying long. In 1932, a foot fell on downtown Newhall. But the big daddy was the blizzard of 1949, when it snowed for almost a week. Drifts of 6 feet were reported above 1,000 feet. The odd thing was that it was warm and drizzly at Frazier Park's 1-mile elevation. (Courtesy SCV Historical Society.)

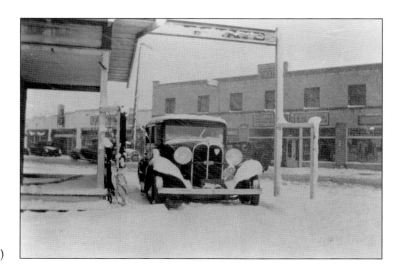

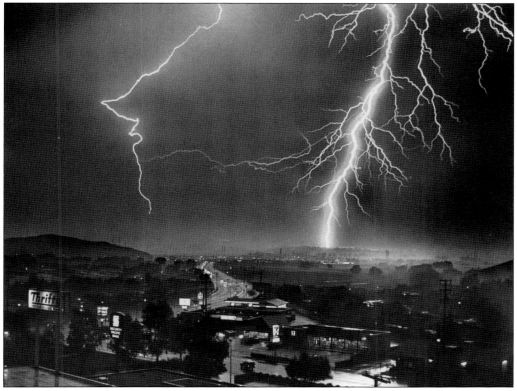

One of the blessings, and curses, of local weather is it stays pretty much the same. Every once in a while, the SCV gets Old Testament rains. In 1969, it rained every day of February except for one. Three full-grown African lions escaped during a flood at Africa USA (today's Shambala). The lions charged the sheriff's deputies in a mobile home park before being shot and killed in a driving rain. (Courtesy SCV Historical Society.)

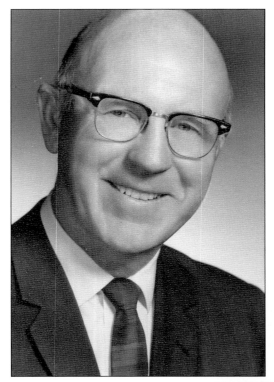

From 1948 to 1965, principal George Harris (left) learned the names of every student at Hart High. He met Ronald Reagan twice. As young men, they crossed paths in sports in Indiana. Reagan spoke twice at Hart High in the 1950s and 1960s, drawing only tiny crowds and a page-8 story in the local *Signal* newspaper. For a half-century, Harris had a profound effect on thousands of local students, remembering every kid's name, including star athlete Joe Kapp (below, later quarterback of the Minnesota Vikings). The Hart Indian would become football trivia, being the only quarterback to take a team to a Super Bowl, Gray Cup, and Rose Bowl. His fullback at Hart in 1955 was future movie star Gary (then, Yurosek) Lockwood (*2001: A Space Odyssey*). It was Principal Harris who taught Joe how to throw a spiral. (Above courtesy Lee Harris; below courtesy Bruce Fortine.)

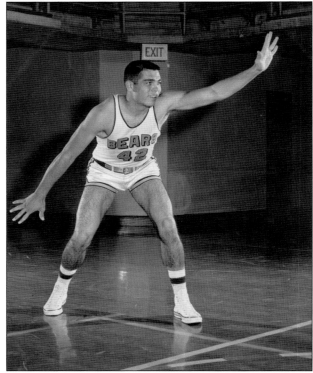

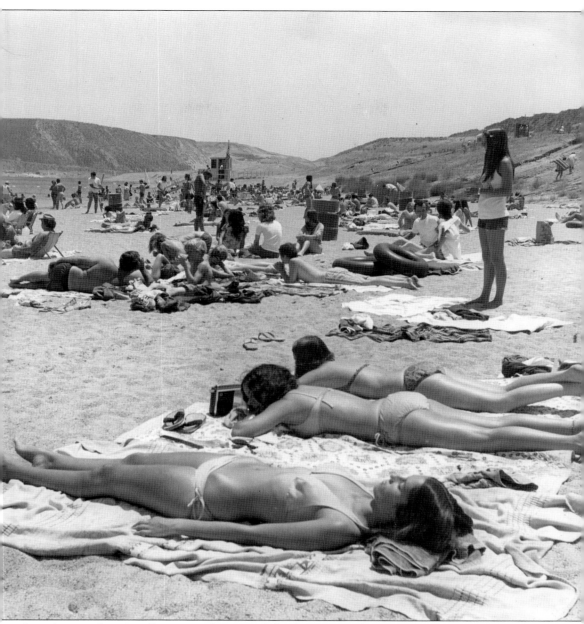

It took more than 1 million giant dump-truck loads to create the 425-foot face of the dam that would hold 32 billion gallons of water—three times the size of the St. Francis Dam. At exactly 10:03 a.m. on January 26, 1972, a switch at the Edmonston pumping station south of Bakersfield was thrown and water began pumping. The first drops of water roared through the massive pipeline, headed to fill the new Castaic Reservoir. Despite 2,500 gallons being pumped every second, it would take nearly three years to fill the massive man-made lake. On busy days, the lake will host 15,000 sun and water worshippers. That's quite an increase from 1857 when naturalist John James Audubon camped out to draw migrating wetland birds. (Courtesy SCV Historical Society.)

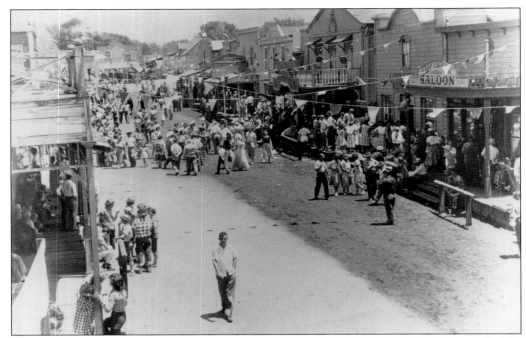

Today Santa Clarita has the Cowboy Fest. In 1950, Melody Ranch (turned into Slippery Gulch) was the scene of perhaps the biggest weekend party ever. As many as 50,000 people would show up for one of California's biggest Fourth of July parades, the rodeo, and festivities at Saxonia Park and Val Verde for the African American celebration. (Courtesy SCV Historical Society.)

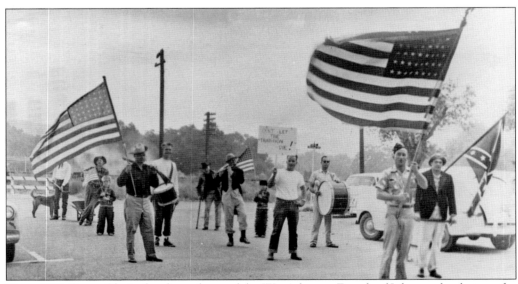

Since 1932, Santa Clarita has hosted one of the West's largest Fourth of July parades, but apathy almost killed the 1955 trek. Without plans or permits, a group of old-timers, led by British war bride Bobbie Trueblood, staged a last-minute celebration. They were quickly joined by hundreds. The local sheriff's captain, driving by, hid his face, pretending not to see the parade so he would not have to stop it. (Courtesy SCV Historical Society.)

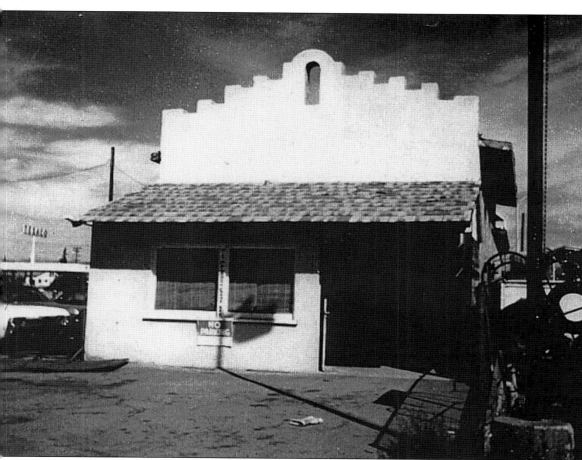

George Herriman's *Krazy Kat* cartoon strip was used on the front page of the 1922 *Los Angeles Times* to describe the original Newhall Jail, seen here. The place was made with the wrong mixture, and crooks could escape just by wetting their finger and boring a hole through the thin wall. Built in 1888 at a cost of $236.25, it was replaced in 1926 by sub-station No. 6 a half-mile east. Cells were added in 1928. The little headquarters had all of huge north Los Angeles County to patrol. Prior to two-way radios, night patrolmen drove by the station. If an outside light was green, everything was okay. If it was red, they had a call. For a while, sheriff's deputies carried pockets full of nickels for phone booth calls. Sub-station No. 6 was the *Signal's* production office in the 1970s and now is a storage room for the Canyon Theater Guild. (Courtesy SCV Historical Society.)

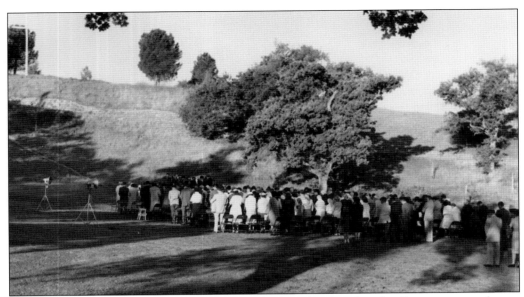

Thanks to a lawsuit by Beverly Hills parents, schools within Los Angeles County were no longer bound to be part of Los Angeles Unified School District. Right after World War II, the William S. Hart High School Union School District was formed and named after the actor. He wanted the school to be named John Fremont. By a narrow vote, the mascot became the Hart Indian rather than the Hart Buckaroo. Above is the ground-breaking ceremony on Newhall Avenue. Hart opened its doors in 1945 to 73 freshmen. Today there are more than 20,000 students in the district. Below is the Honby Men's Club from Hart's class of 1968. The community of Honby was taken over without a shot fired in the 1980s by Canyon Country when they moved their "Welcome To" sign down the road. (Above courtesy A. B. Perkins; below courtesy Hart *Smoke Signal*.)

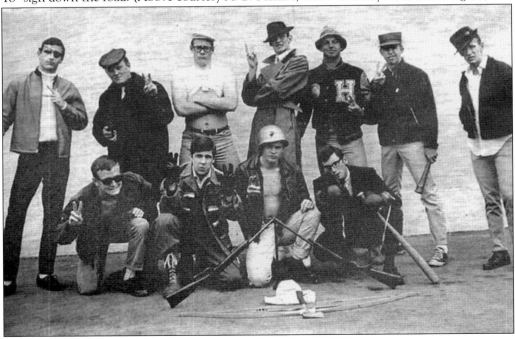

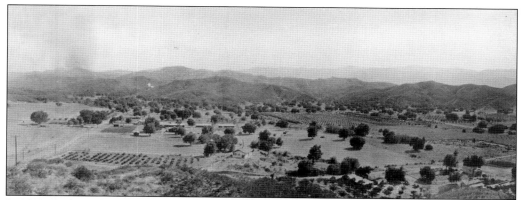

In 1910, Fred Lamkin began developing the farmland south of Lyons Avenue into a residential area of primarily ranchettes. Lamkin had married into the Pennywitt family in Newhall, and one of his sister-in-laws had such a cheerful disposition, she earned the nickname of Happy. They called today's shady enclave Happy Valley after Happy Pennywitt. (Courtesy SCV Historical Society.)

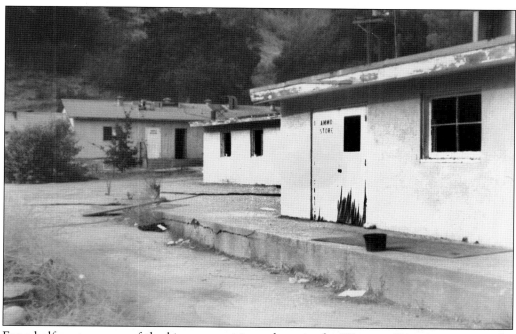

For a half-century, one of the biggest munitions plants in the West was Bermite—next to the rodeo grounds. Heavyweight champ "Gentleman" Jim Corbett bought the hilly area in 1901 and turned it into an explosives factory. Prior to World War II, Pat Lizza bought the grounds and started Bermite—half "Bernie" for his friend/general manager, half "mite" for dynamite. It is the site of the housing development Portabella. (Courtesy Leon Worden.)

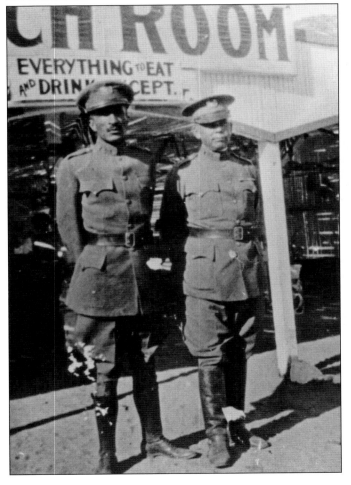

Up until the 1960s, Val Verde, northwest of Castaic, was predominantly an African American community. Founded at the start of the 20th century, it was called Ramona Hills, then Eureka Village and Eureka Villa. These brochures (above) were distributed throughout black Southern California. During an invisibly imposed segregation, tens of thousands of blacks would spend major holidays at the resort dubbed the "Black Palm Springs." Dr. Harry Ted Daily (which is a great name for an editor) ran the local Val Verdian newspaper during the 1940s. Actor James Earl Jones owned a Thoroughbred ranch here. Pictured are March Banks and Major Hammond during a WWII gathering. (Both courtesy SCV Historical Society.)

Where Granary Square sits today, on McBean Parkway, was the Newhall Airport. Locals called it Newhall International because it made a bimonthly mail run to Mexico. Before World War II, the state passed a measure to build Los Angeles International on the grounds. After the war, Newhall Airport moved a bit south and closed in 1947, right after this glider race. Andy Devine, who played Wild Bill Hickcock's sidekick, Jingles, owned the airport in the late 1920s. (Courtesy Russ Magowan.)

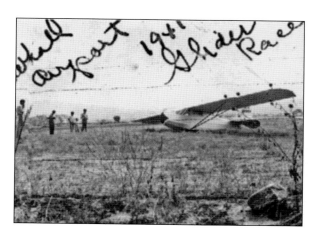

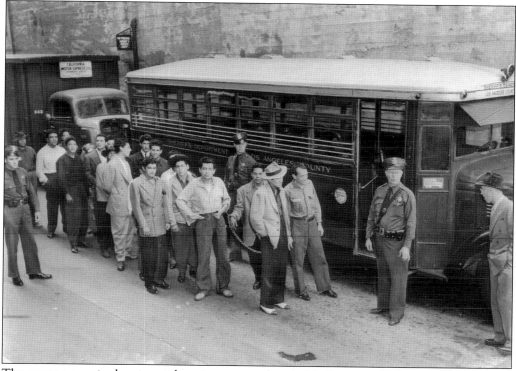

The county exercised eminent domain over rancher A. M. Dunn in the 1930s and turned his beautiful spread into Wayside Honor Rancho. The next day, the sheriff's department "discovered" a huge oil reserve on the property that brought in a fortune. Wayside provided most of the meat, bread, and dairy for the county prison system. Robert Mitchum served there. Unlike this 1940s photograph, today it is maximum security. (Courtesy Los Angeles Sheriff's Department.)

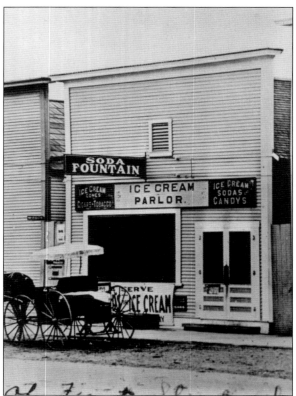

Before Starbucks, there was Woodard's Ice Cream Parlour. The Los Angeles County Library opened a branch in Newhall's dessert shop on March 1, 1916. Christine Woodward was master chef, cook, bottle washer, ice cream scooper, and the valley's first librarian. In the next decade, the library would swell to about 500 titles (200 being magazines). *Signal* editor Blanche Brown would take over as librarian. (Courtesy SCV Historical Society.)

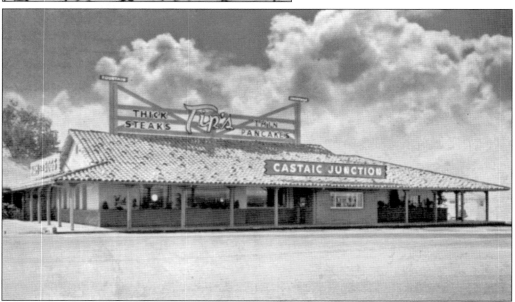

One of the high holy places of eating obligations was Tip's. Originally, it was the Beacon Café and was located at Castaic Junction. It moved to the top of Lyons Avenue, overlooking I-5, and became famous as home to Bobby Batugo, voted the world's best bartender for many years. (Courtesy SCV Historical Society.)

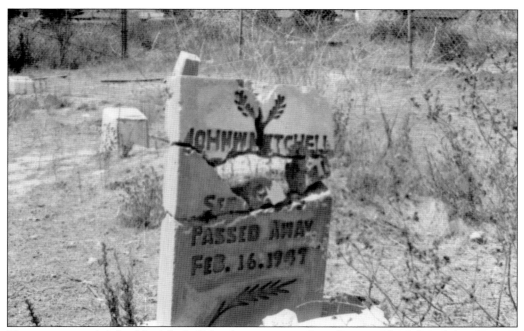

There is not much left of the Mitchell family cemetery in Lost Canyon. Vandals and the elements have destroyed many of the tombstones. There are only two family plots left in the SCV—the Mitchells' and the Ruizes' in San Francisquito Canyon. Witnesses claim both are haunted. (Courtesy SCV Historical Society.)

Many swear that the spirit of Rory MacGregor (there is some debate as to whether or not this man is Rory), a local cowboy, haunts Heritage Junction. The valley boasts of dozens of ghost tales, plus the SCV was the location of Bigfoot sightings in the 1940s and a huge Bigfoot hunt during the 1970s. (Courtesy SCV Historical Society.)

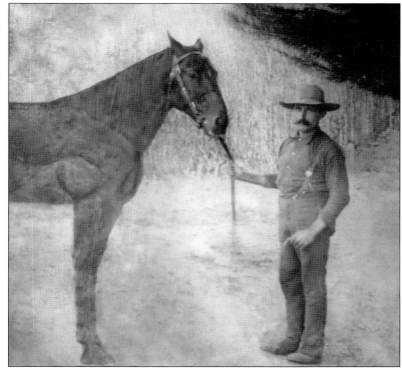

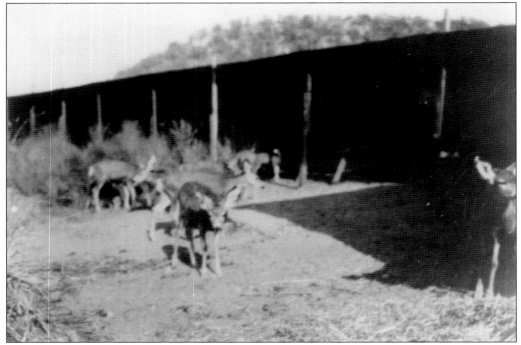

Leisure had a more tranquil feel in the early 1900s. Remi Nadeau III was grandson of Remi I, who was one of Southern California's most powerful men. Remi III built a fabled deer picnic area and tourist attraction in Canyon Country, collecting 90 percent of earth's deer species before a disease swept through the park killing most of his stock. (Courtesy SCV Historical Society.)

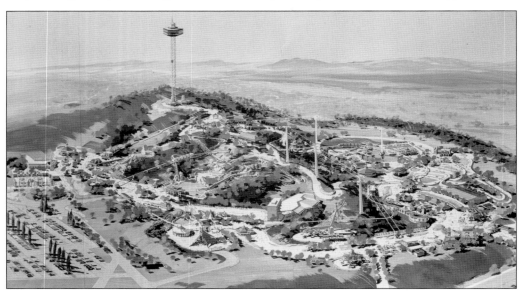

Two odd partners—Sea World and Newhall Land—joined up to open Magic Mountain on Memorial Day 1971. The 200-acre amusement park would be sold in 1978 to Six Flags. With its 384-foot tower and home of Bugs Bunny, it became, for better or worse, the new and forever identifying landmark of the Santa Clarita Valley. (Courtesy Newhall Land.)

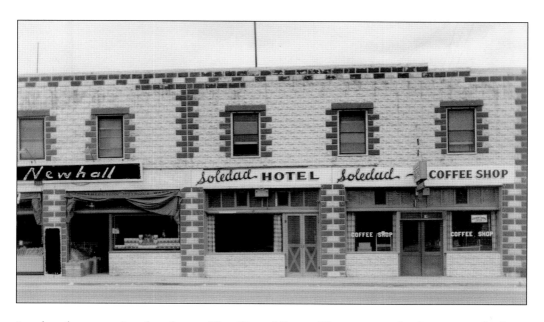

Landmarks come. Landmarks go. The City of Santa Clarita is involved in a stretched-out redevelopment of downtown Newhall. Above, at the corner of Ninth and Main Streets used to sit the spiffy-looking Soledad Hotel. Before that, it was Frances Phillips's boardinghouse, and before that, it was the early home of Standard Oil. When they razed the building in 1951, locals were amazed that the two-by-fours actually were 2-by-4 inches. Today the heart and soul of the old part of town is the little coffee shop, the Way Station, a unique eatery that serves wide, rolling expanses of beige breakfasts. (Both courtesy SCV Historical Society.)

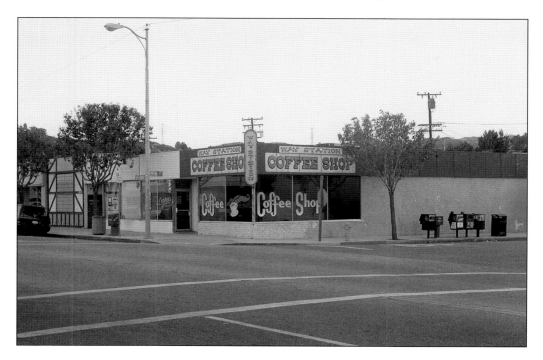

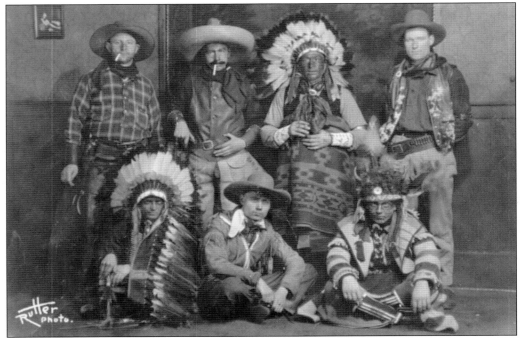

Part of our heritage is naturally who is climbing about our family tree. That dangerous-looking saddle-pal in the top row, far right, is Clyde Hamilton Smyth, a bronco rider who competed at the Hoot Gibson Rodeo Grounds in the 1920s. His son would become Hart District superintendent and Santa Clarita mayor Clyde Smyth. Clyde's son Cameron would also become Santa Clarita mayor and 38th District assemblyman. (Courtesy Clyde Smyth.)

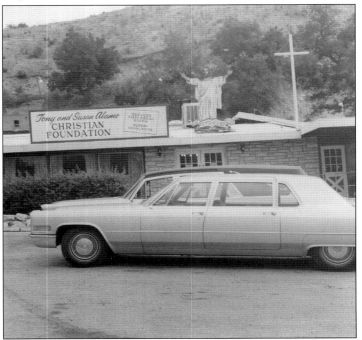

The SCV was famous for another kind of family. Reputed cult leaders Tony and Susan Alamo had their world corporate headquarters in Canyon Country. Tony Alamo, also known as Bernie LaZar Hoffman, served time in prison for income tax evasion. The Alamos spent years embroiled in charges ranging from polygamy to child pornography. The Alamo Christian Foundation donated the football bleachers at Canyon High in the 1970s. (Courtesy SCV Historical Society.)

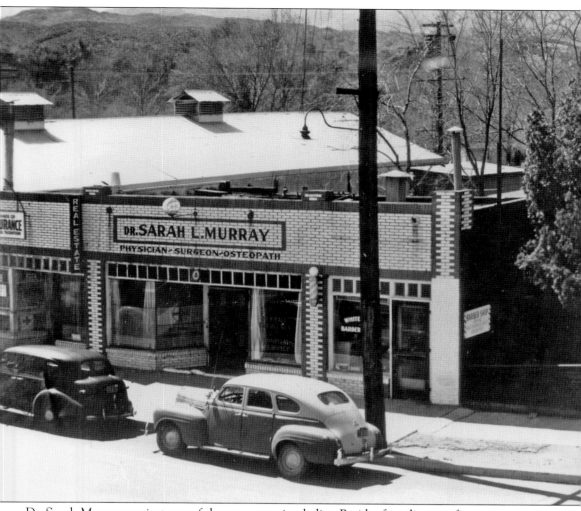

Dr. Sarah Murray was just one of the most amazing ladies. Besides founding our first emergency hospital in 1931 and being a rarity as a female physician, she patented several medical devices, including the still-in-use rolling hospital "bed-desk and table." The Newhall Hospital found itself the center of an odd epidemic in the late 1950s to early 1960s. Around that time, 9 of the 10 top television shows were Westerns. This started a quick-draw craze, and sharpshooters were coming out to the SCV to practice. The top injury in the valley for several years was the self-inflicted gunshot wound. Later the small clinic would be overshadowed by Golden State Hospital, then the sprawling Henry Mayo Newhall Memorial Hospital (HMNMH). Founded in 1975, today it is the SCV's main medical center. HMNMH's very first patient was motorcycle accident victim Sammy Strickland. (Courtesy SCV Historical Society.)

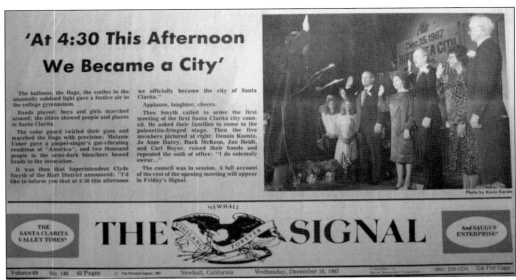

'At 4:30 This Afternoon We Became a City'

The balloons, the flags, the smiles in the unusually subdued light gave a festive air to the college gymnasium.

Bands played; boys and girls marched around; the slides showed people and places in Santa Clarita.

The color guard twirled their guns and marched the flags with precision; Melanie Usher gave a gospel-singer's gut-vibrating rendition of "America", and two thousand people in the semi-dark bleachers bowed heads in the invocation.

It was then that Superintendent Clyde Smyth of the Hart District announced: "I'd like to inform you that at 4:30 this afternoon we officially became the city of Santa Clarita."

Applause, laughter, cheers.

Then Smyth called to order the first meeting of the first Santa Clarita city council. He asked their families to come to the poinsettia-fringed stage. Then the five members pictured at right: Dennis Koontz, Jo Anne Darcy, Buck McKeon, Jan Heidt, and Carl Boyer, raised their hands and repeated the oath of office: "I do solemnly swear..."

The council was in session. A full account of the rest of the opening meeting will appear in Friday's Signal.

Photo by Kevin Korzin

THE SIGNAL

THE SANTA CLARITA VALLEY TIMES®   And SAUGUS ENTERPRISE®

Volume 69   No. 148   62 Pages   © The Newhall Signal, 1987   Newhall, California   Wednesday, December 16, 1987   (805) 259-1234   25¢ Per Copy

By a 2-1 margin in December 1987, local voters created California's newest city: Santa Clarita. In a close vote, Santa Clarita beat out City of the Canyons. Another proposed name was La Mancha, but someone noted it meant "blemish" in Spanish. Two days before the election, bureaucrat Ruth Bennell cut the size of the proposed 90-square-mile city in half. (Courtesy the *Signal*.)

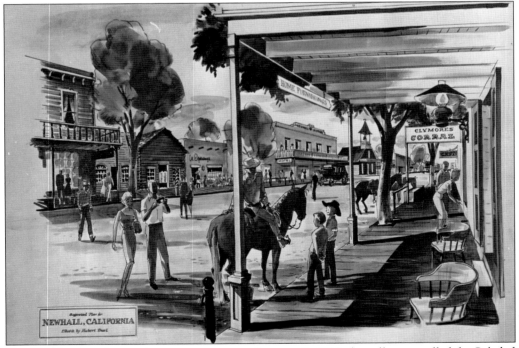

The SCV has been known by many names over the years. In 1938, the valley was called the Soledad Township, whose boundaries covered 1,000 square miles. In the 1960s, citizens attempted to form the city of Newhall-Saugus. An architect composed this plan to turn downtown Newhall into a Disneyesque Frontierland, complete with a 40-foot set of cattle horns hanging over a wooden entry gate. (Courtesy Time Ranger Collection.)

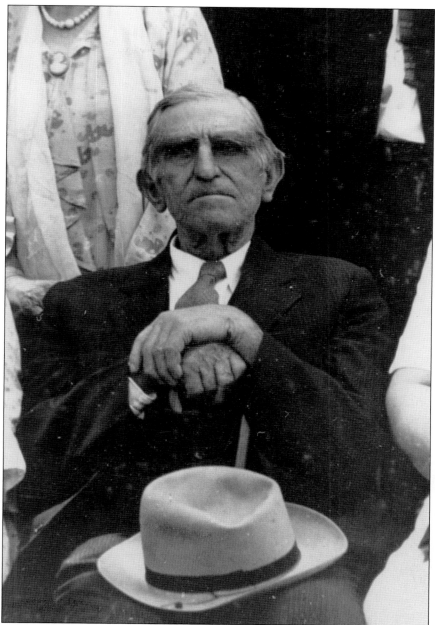

Another presidential candidate was Newhall's native son Henry Clay Needham. During the 1920s, he ran for governor, senator, and three times for the Oval Office as a Prohibitionist. He faired decently overall but never once carried his own SCV. Though he swore off booze, he had a serious sweet tooth. The huge rock portal on Sierra Highway used to be the gateway to his ranch. In the 1890s, Needham was the front man for the Kansas-based Prohibitionists. They purchased 10,000 acres from Newhall Land to start an exclusive non-alcohol-drinking community called the St. John's Tract. Home ownership was tricky. Buyers had to sign an ironclad contract that if anyone were caught drinking on their property, their home and land would return to the seller. There were not too many buyers, Prohibitionists or not. (Courtesy SCV Historical Society.)

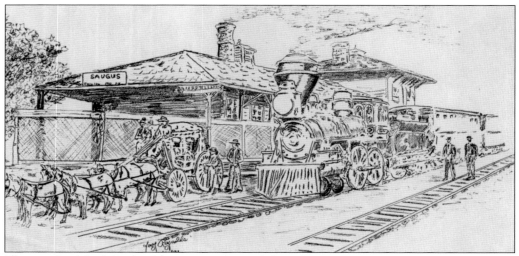

The people of the SCV for the most part fervently love their history, so much so that they moved their Saugus Train Depot. The Santa Clarita Valley Historical Society, nearly 4.5 years old, bought the station from Southern Pacific for $1 to save it from the wrecking ball. They cut it in half, and on June 24, 1980, in the dead of night, they dragged it 2 miles down to the road to inside Hart Park. One inebriated driver was so distracted he crashed into a motorcyclist. No one was hurt. Heritage Junction sits within the park boundaries and contains a treasure trove of local lore and a museum with tens of thousands of photographs and displays. Today several historic buildings also reside in the park within a park. For more information on the Santa Clarita Valley, one may visit www.SCVHS.org. Founded in 1975, the society's Heritage Park is 25 miles north of Los Angeles in downtown Newhall, within the city of Santa Clarita. (Above courtesy Jerry Reynolds; below courtesy the *Signal*.)

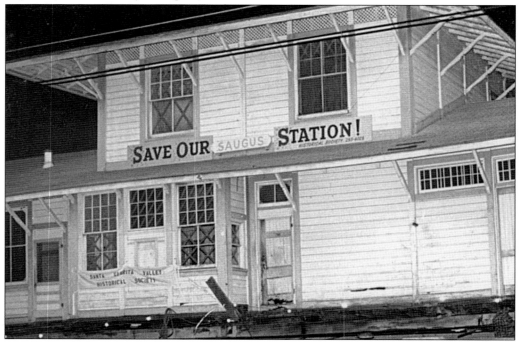

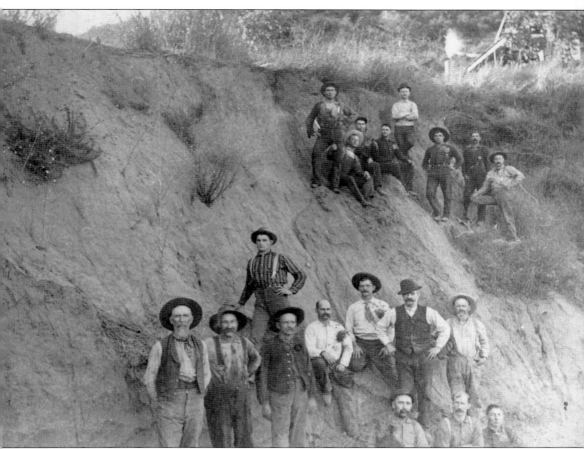

From its Wild West heritage of rough-and-tumble miners, pistol fighters, and outlaws, to a great place to dump homicide victims (Joseph Wambaugh's *The Onion Field* is based on an incident here), the Santa Clarita Valley still has a reputation of being "quirky." Perhaps, this is why: the moon may have come from Canyon Country. Visiting geologists from UCLA in the 1970s noted that the Soledad Canyon area was rich in the rare mineral anorthosite, which is also found on the moon. The mineral—called "Genesis Rock" because it formed part of the Earth's and moon's ancient crusts—was discovered in near 100-percent purity near present-day Sand Canyon and Highway 14. It is more commonly known as plagioclase, a snow-white mineral that almost glows in daylight. It was a stretch, but the visiting rock doctors from UCLA thought there was a halfway-decent chance that 4.6 billion years ago, when the moon broke away from the earth, it came from the northern part of the SCV. (Courtesy SCV Historical Society.)

DISCOVER THOUSANDS OF LOCAL HISTORY BOOKS FEATURING MILLIONS OF VINTAGE IMAGES

Arcadia Publishing, the leading local history publisher in the United States, is committed to making history accessible and meaningful through publishing books that celebrate and preserve the heritage of America's people and places.

Find more books like this at
www.arcadiapublishing.com

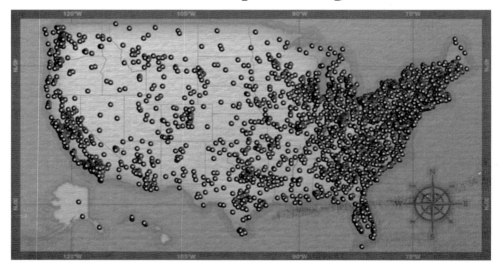

Search for your hometown history, your old stomping grounds, and even your favorite sports team.

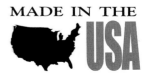